'In Accord'

A history of the Accord Group

CARL CHINN

'In Accord'

A history of the Accord Group

CARL CHINN

BREWIN BOOKS

First published by
Brewin Books Ltd, 56 Alcester Road,
Studley, Warwickshire B80 7LG in 2012
www.brewinbooks.com

ISBN: 978-1-85858-502-4

A Cataloguing in Publication Record
for this title is available from the British Library.

Typeset in New Baskerville
Printed in Great Britain by
T J International Ltd.

CONTENTS

ACKNOWLEDGEMENTS

This is a different kind of company history. Normally an account of a business will be based overwhelmingly on documents, newspaper cuttings, minutes and other written material – supplemented by the occasional interview. In the case of the forerunners of the Accord Group, however, there is a dearth of documentary evidence. This meant that the main, and often, the only source for this history became interviews with or written memories from people who have long associations with the Group's various entities.

This approach did present a difficulty. Should those interviews and memories be edited, paraphrased and mediated through me, the author? It would have been much easier for me to write the book this way rather than painstakingly transcribe the whole of an interview of an hour or more; but I decided that it would be wrong to do so. Instead I felt that the contributions should stand in their own right with some stylistic, grammatical and textual changes agreed with the contributors.

I took this approach for two reasons. First, I believe passionately that every person has made their mark upon history and that each and every person has a story to tell – not only about themselves but also about the people who came before them. History needs to be democratised as the lives of supposedly 'ordinary' people matter because the people themselves matter.

There is much to be gained by encouraging people to tell their own stories and not having them mediated through the words of others – and this belief leads to the second reason for the approach to this history. The Accord Group is dedicated to meeting need, whether that be housing need, employment need, health need or whatever need. It is an organisation that is predicated upon a desire to strive for social justice and on a conviction to give its tenants a meaningful voice. Those principles are made the more powerfully clear by the words of those who have contributed so much to the battle for social justice, empowerment and inclusiveness.

I feel strongly that the interviews and memories included in this book emphasise both a democratic approach to history and make it more personal, passionate, accessible and informative. I feel as strongly that through their contributions, each of the contributors has made a vital impact in the fight to make our society more open and egalitarian. I thus thank them individually and collectively; and for their support and help I also thank Claire Barratt, Director of Communications; Dawn Hendon, Business Support Manager; Claire Morrall, Senior Press and PR Manager; and Daniel Berry, Graphic Designer.

FOREWORD

This history of the Accord Group represents, in microcosm, a fascinating account of social housing through the ages. The Group includes almshouse charities which date back to medieval times and the Victorian period; it embraces the work of Margery Fry, the Quaker social reformer; it incorporates several housing associations formed following the powerful 'Cathy Come Home' film and the creation of Shelter in the 1960s; it also includes a couple of cost-rent and co-ownership societies, a secondary housing co-operative and an association which was formed as one of the black and minority ethnic community organisations when there was concern that mainstream housing associations were not meeting their needs. All of these strands of social housing are brought together in the story of Accord.

Bringing the history right up to date, the organisation has recently opened a factory to build modular timber-framed homes, developed in association with a Norwegian co-operative, HedhelmArnybhus, creating jobs and also building highly energy-efficient, spacious new homes. And Accord, with a proud history of providing care and support to vulnerable people, has recently purchased a private sector care company to deliver domiciliary care, primarily to older people, ploughing back the profits to meet housing and community needs. Alongside this, it has opened a range of innovative 'dementia cafés' in the Midlands helping people with this debilitating condition to socialise as well as obtaining really meaningful support.

The ability to innovate has been a hallmark of the social housing sector and the Accord Group's history is a great illustration of this. The way it has evolved and developed is not just highly relevant but essential to the lives of its residents at this time of considerable economic difficulty.

As the wheels of history turn, from October 2012 the remarkable Barrie Blower – founder of the pioneering Caldmore Housing Association in the 1970s, which is now part of Accord – is Chair of the Group. I wish him and his Board, alongside Chris Handy and his team, every success. I send best wishes to all the residents living in the homes Accord has provided. And I commend this history to all those in the social housing sector who will find much to take away from the evolution of this inspiring organisation.

Lord Richard Best, OBE
Chair of Hanover HA and president of Local Government Association

INTRODUCTION

Homes are the building blocks of our communities. They affect our health, our wealth and our opportunities for happiness. Everyone deserves a place they can be proud to call home, and access to good quality, affordable housing can make the crucial difference that enables someone to play a full and active role in society.

Social housing has come a long way over the last 100 years, but many of the fundamental principles remain the same. As a force for social justice, housing associations provide more than a roof over someone's head. They give people a platform for better life chances. The Accord Group is an example of this – a family of organisations where community and improving health and well-being is at the heart of their work.

Housing is critical to Britain's future – the decisions we take today make a crucial difference to the lives of generations to come.

We know that the current economic climate is seeing families struggle to make ends meet and as the Government moves forward with wide ranging changes to legislation, it is clear that it will be some time before the impact of all of this will be fully understood.

Fortunately, housing associations have a proud history of thinking ahead for the long term. As highlighted in the National Housing Federation's *Building Futures* report, housing associations are continuing to invest millions each year in neighbourhood services – things like training, jobs, skills, health and well-being – precisely because times are tough.

In the years to come, I believe housing associations will continue to have a vital role to play – not only as partners in local economic development but also as organisations committed to giving people opportunities and bringing communities together.

David Orr
Chief Executive
National Housing Federation

Chapter One

HOMELESS IN THE SWINGING SIXTIES

Euphoria surged across England as Bobby Moore held aloft the gleaming, solid-gold Jules Rimet Trophy on Saturday 30 July 1966. The English football team had won the World Cup for the first time and the proud captain had been handed the trophy by the Queen herself. Unbounded joy coursed through the tens of thousands of fans at Wembley, an elation that also raced through the millions of people across the land who had watched a thrilling final on black and white televisions in homes pounding with patriotism and passion.

It was a wonderful day in a time of wonder for England. A few months earlier, in April 1966, the influential *Time Magazine* of New York had pronounced that each decade in the twentieth century boasted a city that dominated and defined that period – and for the Sixties, London was that place. Proclaimed as 'the Swinging City', it was the capital of the world for music, fashion, and youth culture.

The trendy and those desperate to be trendy flocked to the boutiques of the famed Kings Road and Carnaby Street. Along them paraded girls with their hair either long and straight like model Jean Shrimpton, 'the It Girl' of the Sixties, or else cut short like Twiggy, another supermodel who was hailed as the 'Face of 1966'. And like these fashion icons, many of the young women wore the daring miniskirts made chic by the designer, Mary Quant.

London's dominance of clothes and hair design was spread globally by acclaimed photographers such as David Bailey and by dashing actors like Terence Stamp – but it burst forth from the power of British pop music and especially from Beatlemania. That fever all but overwhelmed young people from the summer of 1963 when the Beatles' song 'She Loves You' rushed to number one. It sold more than a million copies and thousands of screaming fans clogged the streets and caused traffic jams when the 'Fab Four' arrived at the London Palladium to star in a show.

Soon afterwards, the British group conquered America. On 8 February 1964 they flew into New York to an ecstatic welcome and the news that 'I

Want to Hold Your Hand' was at the top of the charts. The Sixties were now swinging and British pop was set to rock the globe. Two months later the Rolling Stones shocked critics at the Montreux Festival in Geneva with their raunchy style, but they were soon vying with the Beatles to be the biggest band in the world.

Their phenomenal successes blasted pop and youth culture into the headlines in 1964. Mods and Rockers fought bank holiday battles on the beaches of Brighton and Margate; the Beatles released the film 'A Hard Day's Night'; girls 'were real gone' on crimplene as a fashionable material; and ITV brought out 'Ready, Steady, Go!' its first live pop programme, with Cathy McGowan, the 'Queen of the Mods', as its presenter.

Two years later in 1966, and with the added prestige of the World Cup victory, England was envied across the world as a symbol of success, glory, hope and modernity. Yet youthful, fashionable, daring, exciting, and fresh as were the times for many, for others they were desperate days of hardships and homelessness. In a land of plenty too many suffered deprivation through no fault of their own – yet the bitter cry of the poor was unheard because most politicians and much of the media insisted that poverty had been banished from the Swinging England of 1966.

Such people asserted that there were no poor left, only those who were in need. Those who held fast to such flawed terminology failed to address the question 'in need of what?' If many citizens required a higher income, better housing, sufficient fuel, a good education, and healthy conditions in which to live, were they not poor rather than needy? Unhappily such a challenging approach to social ills was avoided by the powerful because they defined poverty by an absolute criterion: an absence of the minimum resources needed for physical survival – resources like food, clothing and basic shelter. In this simplistic view there were no poor people in a developed country and poverty became a distant problem located in the developing world.

Such ignorant attitudes were founded on the misguided belief that the English poor had disappeared quickly after the founding of the Welfare State by the Labour governments of 1945-51. Nobody can deny that this amazing shift in state attitudes and policies transformed Britain for the good by introducing a radical new system of social benefits, whereby money and services were provided to children and pregnant women and to all those who were ill, injured, infirm, disabled, old, and unemployed.

This approach was in sharp contrast to the hated Means Test of the 1930s, which had striven to exclude people from assistance wherever possible. Such a process had been achieved through assessing not only the

Children in a yard of unhealthy back-to-back houses in Birmingham Street, Dudley in the 1930s. Thanks to Dudley Archives and Local History Service.

savings and possessions of applicants for aid but also the incomes of other members of their family who lived with them. The unwanted legacy of the Means Test was fear and shame, feelings which ensured that by contrast the Welfare State would be built upon the principles of universality and need.

Still for all the obvious successes of the Welfare State, the poor did not go away – that goal could have been achieved only through an effective transfer of wealth away from the rich. Deep inequalities persisted in the Swinging England of the 1960s and indeed became more pronounced as full employment slowly ebbed away.

In this heated atmosphere of social change, both social inequalities and the persistence of poverty were 'rediscovered' by campaigning investigators. Of course, the poor did not need to rediscover their poverty or to be told that they were poor; but the upper and middle class, politicians, the media and opinion formers did need to be informed and shamed into action.

Prominent amongst these activists who sought valiantly to publicise the problems faced by the poor was Audrey Harvey. In February 1960 she wrote a Fabian pamphlet with the challenging title, *Casualties of the Welfare State*. It was based upon her experiences as a social worker in London's East End and it focused on two issues.

First she asserted that many of the thousands of people who sought help from the Welfare State were suffering hardship. Even those with decent earnings could have their regular earning cycle disrupted by sickness or another problem and so fall prey to economic misfortune. Secondly, Harvey made it plain that many of those who were most in need were not receiving the help that they required because the administration of welfare agencies and social service departments was too complex and bureaucratic.

Harvey's pamphlet was one of a number of publications that began to shatter the myth that poverty no longer existed. Another was *Income Distribution and Social Change* in 1962 by Richard Titmuss. In it he revealed that behind the official statistics of income and wealth there was a widening gulf between the social classes in their ability to command both income and capital of different types. The theory that the Welfare State had led to a substantial redistribution of income to the working class was shown to be wrong.

In the same year, Dorothy Wedderburn published an article called *Poverty in Britain Today – the Evidence*. Through the use of a variety of official sources on income and expenditure, she made it clear that about 12% of the population was living at or close to the subsistence levels maintained by the National Assistance Board. This was a disturbing figure, for it was one in eight people.

Other works followed, but amongst the most significant was *The Poor and the Poorest*. Researched and written by Brian Abel-Smith and Peter Townsend it was published in 1965 and was based firmly upon a careful analysis of empirical evidence provided by the Ministry of Labour's Family Expenditure Surveys of 1953-54 and 1960. Household incomes in those years were compared with the scale of National Assistance operative at the time. The authors showed that in 1953, 7.8% of the population was living in poverty and that unhappily the proportion was growing – so that, by 1960, 14.2% of the population was affected. This meant that seven million people were living in poverty.

Social inequality continued to offend Peter Townsend and he strove to fight it. In particular he developed the concept of relative poverty following his detailed survey of living standards in the United Kingdom in 1967-69. This research, and more, was highlighted ten years later in *Poverty in the United Kingdom*. It was contentious to declare that whilst absolute poverty might have

A yard of insanitary Victorian houses in Lower Rushall Street, Walsall during the inter-war years. Thanks to Walsall Local History Centre.

gone from England there were still people who were relatively poor. However, Townsend did so strongly and backed his claims with evidence.

He affirmed that 'individuals, families and groups in the population can be said to be in poverty when they lack the resources to obtain the types of diet, participate in the activities and have the living conditions and amenities which are customary, or at least widely encouraged or approved, in the societies to which they belong'.

This conviction that poverty had to be regarded more relatively had influenced commentators before. In their *Condition of Britain* in 1937, G. D. H. and M. I. Cole had concluded that there was no doubt that the lives of the poor were better than in the past, but they added that 'a people is poor whenever it is poorer than it needs to be, in view of the national capacity for the production of wealth. By that standard, Britain today is poorer than China.'

The Coles were contributors to an on-going debate about the condition of England in the 1930s. As John Stevenson and Chris Cook pointed out in their book on *The Slump* (1979), this meant that the issues of poverty, ill health and bad housing were politicised. They remained in the political arena in the 1960s, as did the proposition that each person should have a minimum quality of life as measured by the standards of living of their own country.

Yet if poverty were to be regarded relatively rather than absolutely, it begs the question 'comparative to what criteria?' Critics claimed that such a concept was too amorphous to be of use; that it was subjective; and that it lacked the rigour needed for social scientific research. It was the awareness of such questioning that led Townsend to try to bring objectivity to his belief in relative poverty. He identified a line below which those who lived could be regarded as poor. This threshold was determined by two factors: the first was the income of a household; and the second was the extent to which the members of that unit lacked twelve items on a deprivation index.

This poverty line was as controversial as was the condemnation of English society made in 1970 by Ken Coates and Richard Silburn through the title of their book *Poverty. The Forgotten Englishmen*. It was based on the research they had led in the late 1960s into the working-class St Ann's district of Nottingham. Students had undertaken a wide-ranging door-to-door survey to inquire into the income, living conditions, employment and trade union membership of the local people.

The research brought to the fore the extensive problems that arose chiefly from bad housing and low pay. It revealed that a large number of people lived in poverty amidst prosperity and were missing out on a better life. The investigation into St Anne's also emphasised that the children of the poor were most likely to grow into poor adults because of an inferior schooling and deprivation. It was a poverty cycle that doomed their futures and blighted whole communities.

Coates and Silburn proclaimed that 'a systematic, simultaneous and integrated assault' was needed upon all areas of deprivation. Piecemeal reforms by agencies that had separate bureaucracies could do little. Instead a wholehearted and comprehensive approach was vital. This would involve 'traditional social welfare measures, a properly conceived and heavily redistributive incomes policy, a housing programme and ... the active encouragement of community-action programmes which reactivate grass-roots democratic and collective participation in decision-making at all levels'. It was a radical call for action and social justice that remains to be answered.

'Cathy Come Home'

The social investigators and activists of the 1960s were praised by the acute French observer of English society, Francois Bedarida in *A Social History of England 1851-1990* (1990). He asserted that 'they brought to light great "patches of poverty", a whole unseen and unheard world living below the poverty line'. Their research 'showed with blinding clarity that, in the midst of abundance and state welfare, at least five million people, about 10 per cent of the population, lacked the means for a reasonable minimal standard of living'.

Yet for all the importance of the women and men who 'rediscovered' poverty, it was a harrowing television play on homelessness that shocked the nation with its story of destitution, distress and desperation – and which stirred some into doing something to change things for the better. 'Cathy Come Home' went out on BBC 1 on the evening of 16 November 1966 as one of the Wednesday Plays. It was watched by an astonishing twelve million viewers, just less than a quarter of the total population of the United Kingdom, and it has been acclaimed as the best British television drama ever made.

'Cathy Come Home' told the upsetting story of a young couple, Cathy (played by Carol White) and Reg (Ray Brooks). It begins optimistically. Cathy is a young woman who leaves her small and boring town. Dressed trendily and smartly, fresh-faced and with fashionably cut blonde hair, she hitches a lift to Swinging London as pop music plays in the background.

Cathy finds a job and falls in love with the clean-cut Reg, a lorry driver at her workplace. They marry and with Cathy expecting their first child but still earning, they have two wages coming in and are able to move into a 'really stylish' modern maisonette with parquet flooring and double glazing. All seems to be going well in their lives but disaster strikes. Reg is injured at work and loses his job, whilst Cathy is no longer working because she is looking after her young child.

With too little money coming in, the couple are unable to pay their rent and they lose their home. As they sink further and further into debt their problems mount. Now with two sons and a baby daughter, Cathy and Reg move in with his unsympathetic mother. The tensions build and they go on to a squalid council house. Once again they are unable to pay their rent and they are evicted roughly by bailiffs.

After a time at a caravan site, from which they are driven by an arson attack, Reg and Cathy have no option but to seek shelter in emergency accommodation run by local social services. Here the officials are like all those with whom the tragic family have had dealings: they are unbending, authoritarian and uncaring. Fathers are not allowed to stay at the over-crowded, noisy, and inhospitable hostel. Reg is separated from his family and drifts away from them and his responsibilities as he sinks remorselessly into a slough of despondency.

Pushed out of the hostel by the petty rules and attitudes of officialdom, Cathy hands her elder son to a friend to look after. She ends up disconsolately traipsing round the streets, holding the hand of her younger son and pushing the pram in which lies her baby daughter. Some nights they shelter miserably in derelict buildings. Then one evening she prepares to sleep on the bench of a railway station but the play ends in a deeply disturbing scene when social services forcibly take Cathy's children from her. Hysterical with grief, she is bereft of everything.

'Cathy Come Home' was an indictment of a society that each year allowed 4,000 children to be taken from their parents and placed into care because their parents were homeless. And it was a denunciation of a society where too few houses were being built to provide homes for citizens. Just before the credits rolled at the end of the play, the fact was presented starkly that since the war, West Germany had built twice as many houses as Britain – a telling statement given that the Germans had lost both the war and the recent World Cup.

The main character of Cathy was played by Carol White, who had also starred in 'Up the Junction'. The screenplay was by Ken Loach, who was also

A yard of back-to-backs in Hanley Street, now part of Newtown, Birmingham in 1965. The lavatories, brewus and miskins are on the left. Thanks to BirminghamLives.

the director. Tony Garnett was the producer and Tony Imi was the director of photography. As for the story, it came from Jeremy Sandford. Each person made a forceful contribution to making the play both compelling and disturbing to watch.

Sandford and his wife, Nell Dunn, were from upper-class backgrounds but in 1959 they had moved to working-class Battersea, where they were affected by the verve and resilience of the local people. Influenced by her neighbours and by the women she met when she worked in a sweet factory, Dunn was inspired to write *Up the Junction* in 1963.

A collection of short stories set in South London, it captured the vitality both of the lives and speech of working-class women in a realistic, down-to-earth, and non-judgmental way. Focusing especially on Sylvie, Rube and Eileen, the book showed that these were women who did not fit into the middle-class domestic ideal of perfect womanhood – for they went to work, were sometimes raucous, enjoyed telling stories, and had their own minds.

Two years later, in November 1965, Ken Loach directed *Up the Junction* as a Wednesday Play on BBC 1. It caused a furore as it featured scenes of factory women speaking coarsely and also a backstreet abortion. Mary Whitehouse, a prominent opponent of social liberalism, accused the BBC of presenting 'promiscuity as normal'.

However, the traumatic abortion scene with Rube became a crucial factor in the national debate which led to the legalisation of abortion in 1967. As the unfortunate young woman went to the illegal abortionist, an interview with a doctor was included. He talked of the urgency of changing the law to prevent the '35 deaths per year that we know are directly attributable to the back street abortions'.

'Up the Junction' brought together Ken Loach as a director with Tony Garnett, who was then a story editor on the Wednesday Play. Garnett knew that the play would cause uproar and he played a vital role in supporting it against management opposition and in ensuring that it was broadcast. He also fought for Ken Loach to have the freedom to film not only in a studio but also on location – a new and revolutionary concept.

Loach's realistic approach was developed further in 'Cathy Come Home', for which Garnett was now the producer. Some scenes were improvised and others included members of the public – some of whom were extras and some of whom were unaware of their inclusion. Loach's determination to give a voice to working-class people was enhanced by the inclusion of urban sounds and by the way the fictional narrative was interspersed with voiceovers from factual interviews of people describing the appalling housing conditions they had suffered.

'Cathy Come Home' was mostly filmed on location by Tony Imi. Innovatively, he used a hand-held camera to take moving action shots and close ups. This style ensured that the play was not only grittily realistic but also that it had both spontaneity and the feel of a documentary.

Homelessness in London

As for the story of 'Cathy Come Home', that had emerged from another close bond with 'Up the Junction'. Its writer, Nell Dunn, and her husband, Jeremy Sandford, were determined to shed the shackles of class prejudice and do good for those who had not been as fortunate in their lifestyle as they had been. In Sandford's case, he became an activist against homelessness, a campaign that he was pulled into by a personal experience that shocked him.

When he and his wife were living in Battersea, they became aware that a neighbour and her children had been evicted and placed in Newington

Lodge in Southwark. This was an accommodation centre for homeless families and operated by London County Council Welfare Department, but it was a place that resonated with heartache and hurt for it had been built in 1850 as a workhouse.

Huge, brooding and prison-like, workhouses were hated as the bastilles of the English working class, symbolising their oppression as much as had the Bastille prison in Paris for the working people of France. They were entered through what were known as Archways of Tears. No wonder. The poor stepped through them as a very last resort, aware that all that awaited them was humiliation, indignity, harshness, sorrow and suffering.

Inside husbands and wives were separated and sent to different sections, whilst daughters were taken away from their mothers and sons from their fathers. All were stripped, washed and put into uniforms and then given work: picking oakum, breaking stones for roads, and horticultural work for the men and older boys; and washing in the laundry, sewing and cleaning floors for the women and girls.

The only way to escape was for an 'inmate' to show that he or she could support themselves outside. Perhaps younger people could do that, but the old had no chance. Once they had passed through the Archway of Tears, they were condemned to a life sentence and when they died, they were subjected to the greatest indignity of all – a burial in a pauper's grave.

From 1861, the workhouse in Newington was used as a poor law infirmary and from 1930, with the abolition of the workhouse system, it became Newington Lodge Public Assistance Institution. This function supposedly ended with the coming of the Welfare State in the late 1940s, but this oppressive building continued to be used for housing the most vulnerable members of society.

On 1 December 1961, *Time Magazine* reported that it held '266 women and children from 72 fragmented families'. The article in which these figures were included was entitled 'The Front Door Famine' and it emphasised that 'in the midst of Britain's unparalleled prosperity, many thousands of low-income families have never had it so bad. These are the "decent, ordinary people," in the words of one social worker, "whose only problem is that they can't find a front door".'

Time Magazine revealed that each day in London alone, seven families became officially homeless. Most of these ill-fated people were young couples with several children. Despite a vigorous programme of council housing, they were unable to find accommodation as there was a massive housing shortage. This meant that private landlords were able to charge high rents for single rooms to childless tenants – whilst 'for a dingy, three-room basement apartment without private bath or kitchen (they) can usually get far more than a working-class family can afford'.

These observations substantiated those of Sandford, who by now had become an assiduous researcher into the problem of homelessness and an advocate for the homeless. In an article entitled 'Families Without a Home', published in *The Observer* on 17 September 1961, he noted that each day three families in London were made homeless 'in the sense that they had nowhere else to sleep but the street'.

They had been made homeless 'because accommodation could no longer be found on the open market by an unskilled worker who is a family man'. Families who lived in council flats and those with controlled rents were still paying rents that they could afford but 'outside this charmed circle' there was nothing. Private landlords could be choosy and they did not choose families with children.

In his penetrating article for *The Observer*, Sandford described his visit to Edna, his former neighbour, at Newington Lodge. He was appalled with what he saw. Up to three families were crammed into one room that contained up to thirteen beds. Husbands were excluded and had to find other accommodation. Edna and her children shared two toilets with another 64 people. They ate food at long tables in a communal dining hall, and 'owing to the number of inmates who contract dysentery, new arrivals must queue up three times for the unpleasant ritual of "swabbing" up the backside'.

Edna had been told by the doctor at the institution that as there was dysentery in the walls she must keep her children as clean as was possible. She heeded the warning and at first locked the children in their room to make sure they stayed healthy. But Edna was paying the LCC the sum of £5 19 shillings (just under £6) a week for bed and board, whilst her husband had to pay for separate lodgings as well as for national insurance, the storage of their furniture, travel and clothes. So rather than starve, Edna had to take her children into the communal dining room. She discovered that high tea, the last meal of the day, was scanty fare of one piece of cheese, tea and two slices of bread – or else a piece of jelly, tea and one slice of bread.

The chief welfare officer of the London County Council told Sandford that over 20,000 families had passed through Newington Lodge since the war and stressed that 'the days are past when your homeless family was in any sense a "problem" family. These days the people who come here are all decent people, victims of the current housing crisis whose only problem is to find a home of their own.'

Despite this realisation and despite the fact that the women had to pay for their food and board, the women were treated without respect. The official policy was based on 'disincentive' – to make the Lodge so unappealing that the women would be forced to move on quickly. Out of the 25 families who arrived each week, only five or six would remain a month later. As for the others, 'by hook or by crook' they squashed themselves in somewhere or else, as Sandford put it so graphically, they moved into 'a never-never world of institutions and workhouses, living often for years on illusory hopes of housing'.

If a woman had not gone within a month, the authorities 'asked' her to leave to make room for new admissions. With nowhere else to go, they and their children slept in parks and railway station waiting-rooms until their children were taken away from them because they were deemed as 'in need of due care and protection'. The family had been broken up by a society that was culpable for its lack of care and attention to its citizens.

Edna's plight was all too common. The last time Sandford saw her it was during visiting hours and her husband was also meant to have been there but he did not turn up. Edna had rowed with him after he said he could not bear to set foot in 'this place' and that he could not afford the fares for travel. Quite rightly his dejected wife challenged him by asking 'what about me? I have to live here.' Adding to her woes, two of Edna's children had been taken away in ambulances because they had 'the sickness'. Rapidly losing her confidence and self-esteem, Edna was also losing her husband and her children.

Sandford's exposé in *The Observer* was followed two weeks' later by an investigation by 'Panorama' on BBC 1. There was a national outcry and Newington Lodge and places like it became a national scandal – but few bodies really did anything for the homeless apart from the Salvation Army. Unhappily, homelessness became an almost accepted part of the national scene. It was an attitude that Sandford continued to confront by publicising the trials and tribulations of women like Edna, who thankfully went on to escape from Newington Lodge.

On 23 September 1962 he wrote another article for *The Observer* called 'London's Homeless Revisited' and he went on to write a radio documentary called 'Homeless Families'. In 'bitterness and anger' at what had happened to Edna and women such as her, Sandford then wrote the story of what was to become 'Cathy Come Home'. It was rejected by the BBC for the Wednesday Play, but his wife, Nell Dunn, brought it to the attention of Tony Garnett. He got the play off the ground, whilst Ken Loach joined Sandford in visiting hostels and homeless people. The two men also worked on the script, which changed many times before it was ready.

A few days after it was broadcast, 'Cathy Come Home' was accused of 'sailing under false colours' by Philip Purser the television critic of the *Sunday Telegraph*. He objected to the melding of fact with fiction that was such a notable element of the play. In his review in *The Guardian* on 17 November, Gerard Fay agreed that 'there could be a purely aesthetic argument that it is not really a play but a documentary' but asserted that it was 'much more of the latter'. He went on to state that 'it seems hand-held both in camera work and by microphone; the dialogue is ill disciplined and at points a bit coarse (but life itself is a bit coarse and often ill disciplined).'

Fay proclaimed that 'Cathy Come Home' was first rate for its authenticity and 'some outstanding performances, not just in the set pieces by Cathy and Reg, but in the snapshots of other characters passing'. It had no falsity and 'no doubt there will be a fuss worked up about this play or documentary or whatever we decide to call it'. A fuss indeed there was.

The BBC was inundated by phone calls after its broadcast and two days later *The Guardian* reported that the Local Government Information Office was to present the BBC 'with reasoned views which have been sent in by councils in many parts of the country'. People had complained that the play's innuendoes were unfair to local authorities 'which try so hard to help the genuine homeless'. One of those councils was Birmingham.

Birmingham's Housing Crisis

The objections of Birmingham Council to 'Cathy Come Home' were made the more strident by the fact that some of the street scenes in the play had not been filmed in London – where the story was set – but in Hingeston Street in Brookfields, Birmingham. As in London and other big cities, there was a critical housing shortage in Birmingham; and as with the capital, the older central districts of the West Midland's city were dominated by badly-built, insanitary and outdated housing that was an unwanted legacy from the Victorian age.

The unprecedented population growth of the early to mid-nineteenth century, coupled with mass migration from the countryside, had accelerated the rise of great towns and led to an insatiable demand for houses for workers. Fields, gardens, allotments and plots of all kinds had disappeared under the relentless onslaught of urbanisation led by jerry builders. Small-scale, short of funds and untrammelled by planning regulations, they threw up as many houses as cheaply as possible on as small a plot as possible so as to maximise the return on their investment.

In London these buildings were often tenements; in Birmingham and much of the Black Country they were back-to-backs. Usually erected on impure foundations and built shoddily with inferior materials such as dirt instead of sand for the mortar, a back-to-back was one of a terrace of houses at the back of which was another dwelling belonging to another terrace. Thus two houses shared a dividing wall merely one brick in depth. This meant that there were no back doors or windows. Consequently there was a lack of light and no through ventilation.

All back-to-backs had a small room downstairs which was multi-purpose in its functions, having to serve as a living room, dining room, kitchen, wash room, work room and sometimes a bedroom. Cooking was on a range or latterly, on a cooker placed in a tiny scullery with a crock sink and a few shelves. Sometimes there was also a cellar in which coal and wood were kept for fuel. The flooring of the all-encompassing room downstairs was quarry

Birmingham women in 1966 marching to demand decent homes for their children and appealing to be taken out of the 'pigsties' they were living in. Thanks to the Birmingham Mail.

tiles. This would be covered by peg rugs made by women bodging or podging (stitching) old rags on to urden sacking.

Many back-to-backs were two-storey high, meaning that there were two small bedrooms above the one room downstairs. However, there were a large number of attic high back-to-backs, which gave extra sleeping space by having one bedroom above another. Long terraces of such back-to-backs dominated many streets. Between four or more of these front houses there was an entry which led to what officials called a court but which was known by working-class Brummies as the yard and by Black Country folk as the fode. This gave access to the houses behind the front houses and normally to another terrace of back-to-backs that ran along the yard.

The houses that backed on to these faced into another yard. Each yard was shared space in which there were communal facilities. These included the washing line and the brewus, or washhouse, in which a copper was set in brick and below which there was space to light a fire. The yard also had an area for the ashes and rubbish that was called the miskins; and lavatories – one of which was shared between two or more families.

Back-to-back and up the yard was the lived experience of hundreds of thousands of Black Country folk and Brummies from the early years of the nineteenth century until the late 1960s. Built hard and fast by factories, in neighbourhoods where the light was dowted and the fresh air was sullied by the pollution of industry and the crowding together of buildings, back-to-backs were embedded in a gloomy setting and were blackened by the smoke that was belched out by innumerable factories and works.

Dark, lacking in ventilation, cramped, unhealthy and with a lack of privacy they drew condemnation early on. In 1840, the Select Committee on the Health of Towns, headed by the MP for Shrewsbury, Robert Slaney, called for the banning of the building of back-to-backs and of houses in courts and alleyways without a thoroughfare at each end. A bill to that end was introduced. It fell before the self-interest of a Parliament dominated by property owners who resented any suggestion that their rights should be infringed. Thus the rights of the poor were sacrificed for the motive of quick profits from bad housing.

Recognising the need for better quality homes for the working class and that builders would not provide them unless enjoined to do so, Manchester banned the building of back-to-backs in 1844. Its example was later followed by Liverpool, but in Birmingham back-to-backs were built until 1876, when a by-law effectively forbade them. In parts of the Black Country they continued to appear for a few more years, as they did in Balsall Heath, which did not join Birmingham until 1891, and Aston, which came within the city in 1911.

By the inter-war years, tens of thousands of Brummies still lived in back to backs – despite the fact that Birmingham had built more than 50,000 council houses. This was a total greater than any authority in the United Kingdom. It was a remarkable achievement and yet even such a huge programme of building new homes was not enough to allow the clearance of tens of thousands of back-to-backs that continued to dominate the streetscape of old Birmingham.

After the Second World War, plans were finally enacted to rid the city of this inheritance of bad housing at a time when reconstruction was acknowledged nationally as of the utmost importance. Yet just as after the First World War the dreams of 'Homes for Heroes' had been shattered on the rocks of a severe economic downturn, so too now did the dreams of building the New Jerusalem founder on the rocks of post-war austerity.

With a lack of building during the war, Birmingham needed to construct 30,000 homes by the end of 1953 to meet the fifteen years' normal housing demands that had developed since the end of 1938. On top of this 10,000 homes were required to replace those destroyed or made uninhabitable by enemy bombing. A further 50,000 houses would have to be provided if there were to be an effective clearance programme of what were designated the 'slums'.

The use of this term emphasised the lack of empathy shown by officials and outsiders with the poor. Originally a neutral word meaning an insanitary area of bad housing, it became loaded with negativity, damning the poor as well as their districts as dirty, rough and unpleasant. Unsurprisingly poorer people found the word 'slum' offensive as the great majority of them strove to keep bodies and homes as clean as possible in the most difficult of circumstances. Moreover, many poorer streets were strong neighbourhoods bonded by powerful ties of kinship, matrilocality, endogamy and neighbourliness.

Still, slum clearance was a priority for most councils, but as in Birmingham the building of new homes was painfully slow – most especially for those that needed better homes and had to live in crumbling houses. By 1947 piecemeal demolition of the most insanitary houses and bombing had reduced the number of back-to-backs in the city from around 39,000 in 1936 to 29,000 – a figure to which could be added the 6,000 other homes that had shared lavatories. This total of 35,000 houses included 6,500 that did not have a separate water supply and had to share a standpipe outside, and 417 with neither gas nor electricity.

Unhappily many of the people who lived in such housing were forced to endure their dreadful living conditions for years more, even though the chains of austerity were slowly cut off and the economy picked up in the mid-1950s. Birmingham, along with other cities, was able to increase its rate of building new houses in modern estates on the outskirts of the city. This

My Mom, Sylvia Chinn nee Perry, grew up in a back house in Whitehouse Street, Aston. Here she is in 1956 pregnant with me and with some of her Cotterill cousins, who lived in the house in front of which they are all standing. The entry behind led to the terrace where my Nan and Granddad Perry at 7 back of 6 lived until they were rehoused in 1965 in a new maisonette in Nechells.

allowed the start of the redevelopment of central areas such as Duddeston and Nechells, but soon after came a marked decline in house building.

In 1958 the number of completed dwellings fell to below 2,500 and then to just over 2,000 between 1959 and 1961. As a consequence the number of applicants on the city's housing register rose relentlessly from 50,000 in 1947 to over 70,000 eleven years later. Under pressure from this housing crisis the Council decided that 60% of new municipal homes would be allocated to those who had been made homeless by the clearance of back-to -backs and the redevelopment of the central wards. The remainder would go to those with a high priority, especially to those with large families.

Moreover the Council adhered strictly to a rule of only re-accommodating people who had lived in Birmingham for five years. This meant that many immigrants who were joined by their families were forced into renting rooms in decaying and unhealthy large dwellings that had been turned into lodging houses in places like Sparkbrook and Handsworth.

In response to their dire predicaments, some people took over empty houses or squatted in old Army camps such as on Billesley Common. As for the Council, it reacted tardily and reluctantly, but by 1956 concern was so growing about the problem of homelessness in the city that it had reached a national audience.

On 1 June 1956, *Picture Post* featured a photograph under the heading of 'Homeless in Birmingham'. It showed Mr and Mrs H. J. Murray, an elderly couple sitting wearily on bench in a Birmingham railway station waiting room, where they slept as they had no home. After an eleven years' tenancy they had been evicted from their lodgings through no fault of their own. Another *Picture Post* photograph showed them waiting patiently to be interviewed at the Birmingham City Council Housing Management and Welfare Offices.

The next month, on 17 July, the issue of homelessness in Birmingham was raised in Parliament by Percy Shurmer, the Labour MP for Sparkbrook. He was a longstanding and staunch fighter for the rights of the working class and he asked the Conservative Government's representatives if it were:

> right to encourage landlords to hang on to houses for sale, hundreds of which are standing idle in Birmingham, when hundreds of families are homeless through eviction and thousands of people are on the housing register in Birmingham? Should not these houses be let to these people? Will not the Minister take some action on a matter which is stirring the conscience, not only of the Churches and the political parties, but of the whole of the people in Birmingham?

As Shurmer stated, churches and voluntary welfare associations were becoming increasingly worried over the plight of the homeless and in August 1956 they set up the Birmingham Emergency Accommodation Bureau. It was supported by the Anglican Bishop of Birmingham and its secretary was Wallace Lawler, a vigorous housing campaigner and later a Liberal councillor and MP for Birmingham Ladywood.

At the end of the month, on 30 August, the distress of the homeless in the City was publicised nationally by Nesta Roberts in a revealing and deeply-informed article for *The Guardian* headed 'The Homeless of a City: In Birmingham at Night'. She made the point that the Council had built 30,000 homes since the war and hoped to build the same number by 1970 – yet with 63,000 applicants on the housing list homelessness was a real problem.

Amongst them was a young couple. The husband was a rubber moulder and his wife was six-months' pregnant. Having no home, one night they would walk the streets and the next they would board an all-night bus to its terminus and then catch the return to the city centre. The couple and their four children had been evicted from their furnished rooms – for which they had been paying a rent of £2 12s 6d (£2.62p) a week, on top of which they had to find the money for gas, food, clothing and other expenses. The landlord wanted to sell the properties and as a first step was getting rid of tenants who were expecting children.

Roberts explained that after their eviction, the wife went to the Council's housing office. Foretelling Sandford's exposures of homelessness in London and the problems of Cathy, this Birmingham woman was anxious about her four children. Two of them were with her mother but the other two were in care and 'she was beginning to despair of seeing the family reunited', whilst she was fearful of them growing up away from her and her husband.

In the midst of a post-war boom in jobs that was drawing immigrants to Birmingham from Ireland and the Caribbean especially, there were many who were losing their homes. *The Guardian* journalist cautioned that it would be wrong to conclude that city's streets were 'nightly seething with families with no roofs over their heads' – but that it would be more wrong to minimise the individual human misery that often extended over years.

Matters were made worse by the inadequate facilities provided to the homeless by the Council. Birmingham had only 70 beds in night shelters for women and children – and fathers were not allowed to join them. These hostels had been set up originally by the Welfare Department to provide one night's temporary accommodation for people who had suffered an unforeseen calamity. Now they were swamped by those who had no option but to settle as long as they could. During winter the women and children were allowed to stay inside throughout the day – ill-suited as these shelters were for anything else but as dormitories.

This paltry provision meant that families were turned away each night. Others were picked up by the police and at least they were found shelter by the Salvation Army. Nesta Roberts stressed that such people were not to blame for their unhappy circumstances. Most had not been evicted either for rent arrears or mismanagement. Instead, having paid extortionate rents for sparsely furnished rooms, many tenants were forced out by unscrupulous landlords at any opportunity they had of renting to someone else who would pay more.

Thousands more of the homeless had been living in overcrowded conditions with family, but had been pushed out by friction caused by a lack of space. The inevitable consequence for many couples was that they had to split up. One such had been apart for over three years. The man had to live with his mother whilst his wife and their children lived with her mother. As he was a night-worker, he could only meet his wife of a weekend.

This photo of a terrace in Cook Street was taken in 1968. The women in view have a petition complaining about their bad housing conditions. Left to right are Mrs Oldacres, Mrs Levy, Mrs Blakemore, Mrs Lamb, Mrs Keane, Mrs Devlin and Mrs Bell. Thanks to the Birmingham Mail.

Personalising the problem of homelessness was a particular strength of the report by Roberts in *The Guardian*. She described the conditions endured by one Irish family. The two oldest boys had been sent to Ireland to live with their grandmother. As for their mother, father and four siblings, they slept crossways in a double bed in a room that was just ten-foot square and yet for which they paid £2 a week.

The Birmingham Emergency Accommodation Bureau was determined to tackle such iniquities by co-ordinating the work of the Birmingham's housing improvement trusts – the forerunners of housing associations; by employing a band of trained social workers to investigate claims; and by appealing to householders who did not normally let rooms to do so to homeless families.

However, many elderly and lone tenants of large houses were unable to respond positively because they were forbidden to do so by their landlords, who would not allow the tenancy of families because they would secure a higher sale price for a property with vacant possession. As a result the Bureau aimed to raise £10,000 to buy a large house to accommodate the most desperate cases.

With such an outcry locally and nationally, the Council was also forced to act. It placed all accommodation for the homeless under the Housing Management Committee and increased the number of its 'half-way' houses. These were small units with shared facilities but such a response was still inadequate.

By 1960 there were nineteen of these half-way houses that gave shelter to just 300 people, whilst 40 women and children could be accommodated in five hostels. The Committee had now made it clear that the cramped conditions in the hostels and the exclusion of husbands were to serve 'as a deterrent to many non-genuine or underserving applicants who report themselves as homeless'. The offensive attitudes of the old workhouse system remained.

Birmingham's Council had one other response to the rising waiting list for houses that peaked at over 70,000 applicants in 1958. As it built new high-rise flats, maisonettes and houses across the city so too did it recondition on a short-term basis many back-to-backs in the central areas. Thousands of sub-standard houses were taken over compulsorily by the Council.

Some that were deemed 'Short Life' were to be demolished within five years. Apart from providing a separate water supply where necessary, repairs to these properties were limited to maintaining them to the minimum standards laid down by public health legislation. These urgent repairs and maintenance of a day-to-day nature included repairing roofs, main walls and defective drains, and making the houses wind and weather tight.

'Intermediate Life' properties were those with a projected survival of five to ten years. These dwellings were repaired more extensively by attending to structural problems, and defective roofs, gutters and chimneys. Work on both categories was carried out by about 100 small building firms, with a combined labour force of 1,000 men, at an average cost of £40 to £50 per house. By the end of September 1953 they had given first and interim state repairs to 25,000 houses.

The final category of sub-standard houses was those with a life expectancy of ten or more years. Many of these were used until the end of the Swinging Sixties so as to accommodate families who were waiting to be rehoused in more modern dwellings. Along with some intermediate property, these long-term houses were reconditioned completely. The most common renovations carried out on them were the stripping and covering of roofs, the renewing of gutters and drain pipes, and the rebuilding of badly bulged or defective sections of walls.

Additionally, there was complete internal repair and decorations, external painting, and the repairing of outside water closets and wash-houses. To complement the work of renovation and to complete the process of reconditioning, the Council also improved the properties. This task included supplying each house with a separate water supply; and installing a separate and efficient outside water closet where the dwelling possessed its own back yard – and if it did not, providing an accessible water closet to the standard of not less than one for every two houses.

This policy of soling and heeling, as it was termed officially, was decried as 'slum patching' by its opponents – and by the mid-1960s those back-to-backs that remained had deteriorated badly despite their previous reconditioning. This deterioration of individual properties was made worse by the decline of whole areas because of clearance. Lived-in terraces of back-to-backs stood amidst a scene of destruction. Mounds of rubble were interspersed with rows of partly-demolished houses surrounded by stinking puddles of water, overflowing drains and decomposing vegetation.

The Octavia Hill Method

Such a dreadful landscape heightened the demoralisation of those many families that were made to live in such a vile setting. One of the few people to stand up for the forgotten people of central Birmingham was Canon

Norman Power. His father, Canon W. S. Power, had ministered for ten years from 1926 at St George's, Hockley. It was an area dominated by back-to-back housing, which he recalled as 'a constant challenge to me' in his book *The Real Thing* (1970).

In the early 1920s, the elder Canon Power gave a talk on such dwellings to the men's club at St Anne's Church in the wealthy middle-class suburb of Moseley. They had no idea about back-to-backs and afterwards they discussed how they could help. The suggestion was made to buy some of them, convert them into through houses and provide them with indoor water, gas, and a fan-light window over the staircase so that old people would no longer have to walk up steep stairs in the dark.

Quickly, though, the realisation grew that the scheme was too big for the club and its members so Canon Power was asked to preach to the whole congregation. He did so and £1,400 was raised to buy fourteen back-to-backs and convert them into seven through houses. Each now had its own toilet, where before one had been shared by fourteen. Importantly alternative accommodation was found for the seven families who had lost their homes.

These reconditioned homes were then handed over to Copec, a pioneering housing association that had arisen from the Christian Conference on Politics, Economics and Citizenship (hence Copec) that had been held in Birmingham in 1924. The delegates had affirmed that good housing was a basic need for healthy living and that it was the most important factor affecting the material and spiritual condition of any family.

Inspired by the Conference proceedings, a group of Birmingham citizens came together to do something. They realised that for the foreseeable future many people would remain living in dilapidated homes. Consequently, they aimed to raise money to buy 'slum' properties and put them in as good repair as possible. The policy began in 1926 when nineteen back-to-backs in Pope Street, on the edge of the Jewellery Quarter, were re-roofed, re-plastered, and re-decorated. They were also given new floors, grates, and repaired staircases; and each was installed with gas and a cold water supply.

Copec's committee was also determined to maintain its properties in good condition and to take a personal interest in their tenants. This was particularly true for prominent women members such as Florence Barrow. One of the philanthropic Quaker family that was closely related to the Cadburys, she collected rents for the Society's houses in Nechells and Duddeston that had been acquired in 1926. The same year, Florence Barrow

The reconditioning of a terrace of back-to-backs in Bridge Street West, Hockley in 1965 by the Irish building firm of J. and T. Walsh in the 1950s. Thanks to BirminghamLives.

also interviewed Miss F. Margaret Fenter for the post of assistant secretary and property manager for Copec.

Miss Fenter was a university graduate who had gone on to gain the Social Study Diploma from the Birmingham Women's Settlement. This was a pioneering organisation run by middle-class women that was based in the poor district of Summer Lane and which provided clubs and support for women, boys and girls. Thence Miss Fenter went to London for training with the women who ran the St Pancras House Improvement Society, founded by Basil Lee Jellicoe an Anglican clergyman and housing reformer.

This training was on the lines advocated by Octavia Hill, a highly influential middle-class woman who had been infused by a passion for social and housing reform from an early age. In 1864 she had persuaded her friend and mentor John Ruskin, the art and social critic, to invest in her dream of improving the housing for 'my friends among the poor' so as to make 'lives noble, homes happy, and family life good'.

They bought Paradise Place off Marylebone High Street in London. Just a short walk from Regent's Park it may have been but yet was it an overcrowded and unhealthy terrace where life was the very opposite of idyllic. These insanitary properties were cleaned, repaired, redecorated and improved. The aim was threefold: first, to show that better quality homes for the poor could provide a profitable return of 5% a year from rents; second to act as a catalyst for the betterment of the lives of the tenants; and third, to serve as a good example to be followed by other housing reformers.

These material, moral and social considerations were underpinned by a highly-personal approach to dealing with the tenants. The corner-stone to this Octavia Hill method was the weekly visit by women to collect the rent. Hill believed strongly that educated, single middle-class women should be involved in work where domestic virtues could be applied. Through their role as rent collectors, they were able to check upon the premises and just as importantly they could develop personal contacts with wives and children especially, and so forge personal bonds between the classes. In this manner, these female rent collectors became the precursors of social workers.

After Paradise Place was transformed, Hill moved on to achieve the same positive results elsewhere and then expanded the scope of her activities. Because the houses that were improved had been of the worst type, they were rented by the poor – unskilled men and women who were underemployed or casually employed as well as badly and irregularly paid. These were people who were unable to afford the higher rents of the model industrial dwellings aimed at the well paid and regularly employed of the skilled of the working class.

Through her understanding of the problems faced by the poor, Hill tried to find local employment for her tenants. She also had a tenants' meeting room set up; whilst any surplus above the 5% return was to be disposed of by the tenants. Although they were guided by their landlady, they were allowed to choose what this money was spent on so long as it was on something constructive like a sewing class.

Importantly Hill saw beyond the house to the neighbourhood. She encouraged neighbourliness and social interaction through making playgrounds out of rough land and building halls. These were decorated by those of her friends who were artists and they became the venues for concerts and theatre performances.

The Octavia Hill method spread rapidly via her example, her writings, her talks and the work of women who joined her. Then in 1884 she took on the big challenge to manage a large number of slum properties in south London for the ecclesiastical commissioners of the Church of England. When plans were proposed for the rebuilding of the estates she argued that it should be on a smaller, more domestic scale as opposed to the large and daunting model industrial dwellings. She also pushed successfully for tenants' involvement.

With the increased scale of managed dwellings came the professionalisation of the female housing workers so that by the early twentieth century they were properly trained and salaried. Miss Jeffery of the St Pancras House

Children playing in a yard of reconditioned back-to-backs in Icknield Port Road, Ladywood in 1965. Thanks to BirminghamLives.

Improvement Society was one of them. A pupil and follower of Hill, Miss Jeffery subscribed enthusiastically to the belief that female housing workers had to have a sense of responsibility and friendship to tenants and their families; whilst she also maintained that the provision of good quality homes was a business that should be a service to the community. They were principles that had a profound effect on the housing societies that developed during and after the inter-war years.

Birmingham's Forgotten People

After the coming of peace in 1945, socially concerned Christians continued to reach out to help the poor who lived in crumbling Victorian dwellings. In Birmingham, the most vocal and passionate of them was Canon Norman Power, who shared his father's concerns for improving the wellbeing of the back-to-back Brummies.

During the Second World War the young Norman Power had run a children's club in his father's parish, in an old church hall in Heaton Street, Hockley. He could never put out of his mind the disappointment of the lads when the room had to be closed because it might collapse under the force of enemy bombing locally. The youngsters could not comprehend the issue of safety. All that they could think of was that they had been abandoned and in their anger and dismay they threw stones at Norman Power after he told them the bad news. He could have walked away. He did not and returned to them when the war was over and started the club back up.

Soon after, Norman Power moved to the Immanuel Church, Highters Heath – right on the edge of the city and the Worcestershire countryside – where he became the youngest Anglican vicar in the land. He made good friends there and then at Christ Church, Summerfield, but it was the folk of Ladywood with whom he was the most associated. Canon Power moved to the parish church of St John's in the early 1950s and watched aghast as the planners and developers not only demolished bad housing but also destroyed community spirit.

Almost a voice in the wilderness at a time when Britain was set on becoming a futuristic nation of wide freeways and high-rise flats, Canon Power called out for both a change of thinking and policy. He agreed that outdated and insanitary housing with communal facilities had to be swept away but he wanted them replaced by houses and not tower blocks in which residents were isolated from each other.

He also argued that, wherever possible, local people should be allowed to rent the new properties in their own neighbourhoods and not be exiled

The Forgotten People of Canon Norman Power: a young mother chatting with two older women in a yard of boarded up and lived-in houses in Alexandra Street, Ladywood in 1967. Thanks to BirminghamLives.

to new towns or distant estates. And Canon Power also stressed that because not all of the old housing was unsound it should be refurbished and not cleared.

Through his weekly columns in the *Birmingham Mail* and in his challenging book *The Forgotten People* (1965) this campaigning churchman pushed forward his sensible and thoughtful ideas. Unhappily his refreshing and informed call fell upon deaf ears. Birmingham was driving forward with its dream of becoming an American-style city and Ladywood, like the rest of central Birmingham, was transformed. As the bulldozers ravaged the historical landscape so did it became a rotting wasteland of empty buildings, rubble, litter, overflowing drains, and broken sewerage pipes. Amidst this devastation the remaining residents had to live.

Yet Cannon Power's urgings were heard by some. In their 2012 report into 'The Voluntary Sector in Transition: changing priorities, changing ideologies', Terry Potter, Graham Brotherton and Christina Hyland emphasise that 'faith-based organisations were also at the heart of the housing association movement'. Inspired by the writings of Canon Norman Power, 'these new housing associations would seek to put the needs of people before the whims of the planners'.

Amongst the societies that would take on these challenges was the Moseley and District Churches Housing Association. Now part of the Accord Group, it was formed by socially-concerned Christians in 1966, shortly before the broadcast of 'Cathy Come Home'. Another similar society was Walsall and District Housing Society, which merged with Parklands in the early 1990s, and was a faith-based organisation also set up by concerned individuals in the wake of 'Cathy Come Home'.

Reactions to 'Cathy Come Home'

The large scale both of Birmingham's housing crisis and its homelessness problem had attracted unfavourable national, regional and local attention. Given these factors it is understandable why Tony Garnett and Ken Loach decided to film some of the street scenes in Brookfields. This poorer working-class neighbourhood was next to Ladywood and the parish of Canon Power, and was included in the Ladywood Parliamentary constituency. In particular, the producer and director focused on Hingeston Street.

Developed from fields by the 1860s, many of its terraces of back-to-backs were named after places in India. There was a story that this was because the builder was keen on Rudyard Kipling's books set in India, and in one of them there was supposed to be a character called Major or Colonel

Hingeston. This story was unfounded as Hingeston Street had emerged decades before Kipling became famous. Instead Indian terrace names like Seringapattam and Poonmallee recalled either sieges by or forts of the East India Company.

Such names may have cast an exotic aura over Hingeston Street: the reality was very different. It was one of the streets where many back-to-backs had been reconditioned and into which homeless families had been moved. Their houses were rapidly becoming uninhabitable, despite earlier improvements, and they stood in an increasingly inhospitable setting. Unfortunately it was a fitting place for filming scenes about the plight of the homeless.

Carmelita, Christine, Roselyn, Everton and Priscilla Jacobs in their yard in Hingeston Street, Brookfields; thanks to the Birmingham Mail. Spotlessly clean, they are off to school – having to pick their way through rubble and rubbish to do so. Their home was the only house occupied in a terrace of ramshackle buildings. Fortunately, the day on which this photograph was taken was the last in which the Jacobs had to put up with life in a small, back-to-back with no hot water and the lavatory down the yard. That afternoon they set off for a five-bedroomed municipal home in Lozells and 'were full of praise for Birmingham Corporation for giving them hope for the future'.

Back-to-back houses were unknown in London, and this feature along with the inclusion of local people as extras and of actuality recording from Brookfields made it clear to some Brummies that parts of 'Cathy Come Home' had been filmed in their city. In the fortieth anniversary year of the screening of the play, its connections with Birmingham were made plain by 'Inside Out – West Midlands' (23 October 2006).

The programme included an interview with Tony Garnett who remembered that local people 'were just marvellous, the way they just didn't hinder our filming – they were very supportive all the way through'. He added that 'that the people we are making the film about are the experts, not us, so the whole crew would consult local people here, and if they said it wouldn't be like that, then we'd listen and change things'.

Back in 1966, however, Sir Francis Griffin, the Conservative leader of the Council, dismissed the play's portrayal of homelessness and housing in Birmingham as 'selective and inaccurate', and in early December leading councillors engaged with Sandford and Loach in a discussion at the Birmingham and Midland Institute. They were attacked by Alderman Dr Louis Glass, the Conservative chair of the Housing Management Committee, for 'sneaking into a Birmingham hostel to get information for their play'. He also deplored the way that the production 'had smacked in the face every agency dealing with the homeless'.

Given the dire situation of the large numbers of homeless people, it would be tempting to regard men like Griffin and Glass as inactive. It would be wrong to do so. The Conservatives had only regained power locally from Labour in May 1966, a few months before the broadcast of 'Cathy Come Home'. And as it was, the two parties shared a post-war consensus that Birmingham had to build as many municipal houses as it could as quickly as it could. In this praiseworthy aim both Conservative and Labour leaderships were beset by difficulties.

The most critical was that despite building tens of thousands of homes, the City could not construct as many as were needed. Birmingham had tens of thousands of applicants on its housing register; it needed to clear its slums urgently; it was running out of land; and its population was growing markedly because of a high birth rate locally, immigration from the West Indies and Ireland, and migration from Scotland, Wales and the north of England.

Of course, such realities were of no comfort to the homeless – but it would also be wrong to see Alderman Glass and other leading councillors as unfeeling. Glass himself was a general practitioner in Ladywood and was highly esteemed for his care and support both for his patients and the local people in general over many years of practice.

Indeed, as a leading member of the Birmingham Jewish community he believed in the sanctity of the family. Consequently soon after 'Cathy Come Home' was broadcast, Alderman Glass announced that the splitting of families in the city's hostels would be ended within two years. He was true to his word and acted even more quickly than he had promised. On 22 January 1967, Colin McGlashan wrote an article called 'No one wants to know about the homeless' for *The Observer*; in it he included the information that Birmingham had just announced that it would now cater for husbands as well as wives and children in its hostels.

The Council also increased the scale of council-house building and of slum clearance. Despite these actions, families were still living in decaying and insanitary back-to-backs until the end of the Swinging Sixties. Amongst them were Mrs and Mrs Jacobs and their eight children. They had left St Kitts in the West Indies in 1965 and at first had lived in lodgings in Sparkbrook.

Here they had stayed for year, until they were thrown out by their landlord who wanted the accommodation. At this time, the Corporation had more than 45,000 people on its waiting list for a property. The Jacobs found a crumbling house in Hingeston Street and by the autumn of 1969 they were one of only four families surviving in the neighbourhood which was in the throes of demolition.

There were about a dozen children left locally and according to the *Birmingham Evening Mail* on 3 September, 'in the jungle of 1,000 hazards' these little ones 'played beneath the forbidding red "Danger" signs'. Mrs Jacobs told the reporter 'of her disillusionment with modern Birmingham, of her constant worries for the children's safety amidst crumbling houses'.

That same year, 1969, Save the Children sponsored an amateur film on slum clearance. Fourteen minutes long and called 'Our Generation' it was directed by John Beacham and Malcolm Dick. Both men wanted to get away from dramatic presentations and their film focused on streets where all the houses were due for demolition but had not yet been fully cleared.

In particular, 'Our Generation' showed children in Ladywood playing amongst half-demolished houses and sometimes near burning debris and it suggested that the wholesale movement of folk into high-rise was causing other problems for children. As was explained in the *Birmingham Post* on 27 May 1969, Birmingham was chosen for the film 'because it is one of the places where the local council has been set upon for its lack of progress in slum clearances. It has a pretty bad record'.

Many in the council would have disagreed vehemently with this interpretation, given that in the last four years of the 1960s it had built a 'world record' 30,000 houses. Yet too many poor people were still homeless or continued to live in dreadful conditions. The last families living in health-threatening back-to-backs may have been moved out by 1970, but the next year any complacency that Birmingham may have had about its housing problem was shattered by evidence from a new organisation called Shelter.

Dedicated to fighting for better living conditions for the poor and for homes for the homeless, Shelter brought out a report with the simple yet striking title of 'Condemned'. It brought to the fore housing problems in five major cities and included shocking photographs of young families and elderly people enduring life in awful housing in Winson Green. Disgracefully, these properties were owned by the Council, and the report damned Birmingham's slums as 'amongst the worst in the country'.

Shelter

'Cathy Come Home' had electrified and horrified the nation. It had thrust the thorny issue of homelessness into the spotlight and ensured a positive reaction not only in Birmingham but also elsewhere. The play was later praised by Anthony Greenwood, the Minister of Housing and Local Government in the Labour Government, which went on to announce a major building programme and to produce a White Paper urging councils to end the separation of parents and children in cases such as that of Cathy herself.

Perhaps more importantly, though, the play had brought massive and positive publicity for Shelter – whose campaign had been launched fortuitously on 1 December 1966, within weeks of the broadcast of the play. According to a report the next day in *The Guardian*, Shelter's aim was to raise £1 million a year by 1970. The chairman of Shelter was the Reverend Bruce Kenrick, founder of the Notting Hill Housing Trust, and he explained that every pound raised by private subscription could do the work of six when multiplied by loans and improvement grants. With £6 million a year available, Shelter could work through local housing associations to provide homes for between 15,000 and 20,000 people a year.

Leading voluntary housing organisations for helping the homeless were co-operating in the campaign and the bulk of the money was to be distributed amongst efficient housing associations which worked closely with local authorities in the four worst-hit cities. These were London, Glasgow, Liverpool and Birmingham – although housing associations elsewhere would also be invited to apply for applications. Some funds from Shelter later went to Moseley and District Housing Association to help its early work.

But 'Cathy Come Home' and the launch of Shelter also acted as the catalyst for the start of new housing associations. Many of them were focused upon the inner city. The back-to-backs had gone but more houses were now decaying. They included long terraces of tunnel-back houses that had been built originally for the well-paid and regularly employed of the working-class in the late nineteenth and early twentieth centuries; and they also included many large late Victorian houses that had been constructed for the middle-class but which had now become rundown lodging houses mostly for immigrants.

The need was great and growing. As early as 4 December 1961, *The Times* had quoted Birmingham's medical officer of health, Dr Millar, as stating that 'conditions in lodgings for immigrants were often infinitely worse than

Serina Gall knocking on a neighbour's door in Tudor Street, Winson Green in 1970; thanks to Birmingham City Council Housing Services. Houses like these in this area were condemned in Shelter's 1971 report. Serina's mother, Barbara Melody, told the Birmingham Evening Mail in 1993 that she and her three children were living with her own parents as well as her siblings. In all 'there were 16 of us in the two up two down house with no hot water and an outside lavatory ... the housing was terrible but the community was great. Everybody helped each other.'

those in slum housing that Birmingham Corporation was demolishing'. Again amongst those housing societies that would take on this particular challenge of bad housing was the Moseley and District Churches Housing Association.

With its vigorous campaigning and hard-hitting approach through the media, Shelter played a crucial role in laying the foundations for the phenomenal growth of what has been regarded as the third wave of housing associations. The first related to the Octavia Hill era of 5% philanthropy before 1914; and the second was focused on the inter-war period when housing societies like Copec were founded to improve housing conditions in older and poorer areas and to press for slum clearance.

Although the third wave of housing associations was mostly associated with Shelter and a call to social action, it drew into it a number of other bodies that had emerged before 'Cathy Come Home'. In 1961 the Conservative Government had realised that there was a need to provide 'for people who do not wish or cannot afford to buy a house although they require no help from the public fund'. Accordingly their Housing Act introduced an experiment whereby the Government would advance money to non-profit making housing associations 'which are prepared to build houses to let at economic rents'.

By this pump-priming method it was hoped that the investment of private capital in housing would be encouraged. As for the scheme itself, it was implemented by the National Federation of Housing Societies, which had been set up in 1935. However, for whatever reasons, existing housing charities tended not to become involved and new associations were set up instead.

In *Three Pillars. The History of the Trident Family of Housing Associations, 1962-2005* (2005), Kevin Gulliver describes how the Templefield Housing Association was begun in 1962 by 'a group of property-based professionals as a vehicle to take advantage of the cost-rent housing experiment'. Three years later the Trident Housing Society was created 'with a mission to develop cost-rent housing, and to explore the development of co-ownership housing, which was promoted by the Housing Act of 1964'. Trident is one of Accord's closest partners.

This legislation had also established the Housing Corporation as the body to stimulate the emergence of housing societies; to handle the funds that the Government would make available to lend to these societies; and to buy land for societies to develop. In his seminal work on *Housing Associations and Housing Policy. A Historical Perspective* (2000), Peter Malpass explains that the Government wanted to encourage 'the formation of societies by groups of property-based professionals, such as solicitors, architects, surveyors, and estate agents, who were allowed to charge their normal fee for work awarded to them in connection with the development and management of houses'.

It seems that some of the roots of the Accord Group are to be found in this sphere of activity in which professionals with a social conscience also saw an opportunity for commercial benefits for their businesses. Parklands Housing Society had strong connections with estate agents and appear to have begun in the mid to late-1960s. As for the Westland Housing Society it was founded in May 1965; it was also associated with professionals in its committee of management; and it moved strongly into the building of co-ownership homes. The co-ownership societies that these associations supported were housing co-operatives designed to give people a step up on the home ownership ladder.

Whatever may have been their beginnings, all housing associations would soon move away from their peripheral role in social housing to become the vital third sector alongside municipal housing and private housing. That notable development is reflected in the growth in size, responsibilities and successes of the Accord Group, which began with the merger of Walsall Parklands with Westlands Homes in 1982.

Chapter 2

MEETING THE GREATEST NEEDS: ACCORD

Dr Chris Handy OBE, Chief Executive of Accord Group

Inspiration in Wolverhampton

There is a 'Cathy Come Home' link with how I became involved in housing in the first place. I was quite touched by that film. Twelve million people watched it in 1966. I was thirteen years old and my whole family watched it. Obviously it didn't hit me immediately but I thought about that later on. After leaving college I got a job with Wolverhampton Council as a professional housing trainee.

Coming from the West Midlands was also very important in my career. I've always stayed working locally. I was born in The Lye, live in Stourbridge, married a Black Country girl, and was a big Wolves supporter. So the attraction of my first job in Wolverhampton was also that I was going to be working in the place whose team I supported. That's a factor that played a big part in choosing a job in Wolverhampton rather than Birmingham.

Some of the first work I did for Wolverhampton was in the homelessness team and I stayed with the Council for about four or five years whilst I was going through the training.

Hilary Clarke was the Housing Director of Wolverhampton Council when I used to work there; she was just extraordinary and inspiring. She had a double first in Mathematics from Cambridge and had an incredibly insightful mind about everything.

Hilary was a highly able woman and like her, very often the members of the Society of Housing Managers were women. It went back to the Octavia Hill connection; initially the managers of housing projects were women in the image of Octavia Hill. Hilary was one of those and as I say she was an inspiring leader.

Part of the work at Wolverhampton Council was to collect the rent and go and knock on doors. I also helped to supervise a number of initiatives. Hilary

Clarke was quite dynamic and she persuaded councillors to do new things that hadn't been tried before in the UK and I helped out. Although you got a bit fed up with the politics, during that time I did work on innovative things like one of the first shared ownership schemes. Wolverhampton was the first organisation in the whole of Britain to do shared ownership in 1972 – part-rent and part-ownership and it really was innovative in its day.

We were again one of the first authorities that really valued tenant engagement in managing their estates. We set up a tenants' group in Heath Town that had a real say in how that estate should be run. I did some work to support that tenants' group in making its decisions and in persuading the Council to do things in certain ways. Hilary Clarke had got these innovative ideas that you might think humdrum now but they were radical then.

There were several of us that were trainees with Wolverhampton Council and we used to talk about housing associations being the future. From 1972 they started getting grants from Government and they were building houses and improving homes. I had a relationship with them because I went on to do some work in housing association houses for the Council and we could see that it was quite exciting work.

Housing associations weren't weighed down by politics – politicians do like telling you what to do, plus officers in local government can simply be functionaries if you are not careful. The housing association world was urgent, immediate, exciting. Out of the trainees, I would say that all but one went to work for a housing association because they were a more exciting place to be.

So I saw a job with Wolverhampton Housing Association and I applied for that. Hilary Clarke tried to persuade me not to leave the Council but it was a manager's role and I got involved with housing associations directly that way. Up until then I had wanted to work in housing aid or homelessness. I wouldn't say it was a direct psychological connection with 'Cathy Come Home' but it was there; I was a person who wanted to do something for the community.

I wanted to go into a job that wasn't just a profession but was doing something to make a difference. I thought it was more about public service. Back in the 70s and early 80s there was still a strong sense of that within local government and even the Civil Service. I think we have lost a lot of that; Hilary Clarke was a particular person who had that public service calling. I wanted to do good and have a good career at the same time.

I got the job in Wolverhampton Housing Association in 1978 and it was small scale, 300 homes in inner-city areas. It was exciting, though, because we were trying things out. It wasn't professional in the way it is now. We would find a property down a street, we'd buy it and improve it and let it. It was all quite fast and we kind of muddled through in a sense. I had a few exciting years there.

For me it was about wanting to do things in the community that I came from and importantly also about meeting need. What we were doing constantly through that time was providing homes and meeting the housing needs of people. We used to talk in those days about meeting the greatest needs, trying to find the person on our waiting list who had the greatest need. There was that link to homelessness as most of the people we helped were homeless or potentially homeless.

Concomitant with Copec

However, Wolverhampton Housing Association was a small organisation. Shortly after I started they merged with Copec, which had emerged originally in 1925. After a few years I became the Housing Director of Copec, before it became Prime Focus and then Midland Heart. Eventually I was the Housing and Care Director in Copec, and that was where I gained knowledge of housing work on a much bigger scale, some 10,000 units back in those days which made it the largest housing association in the Midlands.

Of course, Copec wasn't bigger than Wolverhampton Council, which had 50,000 and more properties, but it was much bigger than Wolverhampton Housing Association. I would say Copec also had a more professional and managerial approach. The real difference, though, between Copec and the Council was that although the Council was quite innovative for a local government authority, it was still quite a slow slog and you could do two or three things and that was about it.

When I went to the housing association sector, those organisations were doing things on the ground. It was exciting, it was immediate, it was urgent. They were able to respond to issues and address them without hanging around from month to month. They'd got agility. And Copec was also very good at lobbying government – and I think Accord is good at lobbying. I think we are quite influential at both a local and a national level and that's down to our senior team. There are a number of people in this organisation that are very good at lobbying and networking.

David Mumford, who was the chief executive of Copec, had joined the organisation when it was quite small and he was another inspiring person. He had a really strong relationship with Sir Dick Knowles, leader of Birmingham City Council, and he taught me to get close, if you can, to key politicians. You were then on their radar and also you might be able to help them shape their policy in a way that benefits your organisation and the people that you are serving.

So David Mumford had created something with his energy and effort and enthusiasm and I wanted to try and do something like that. The opportunity came with Walsall Parklands in 1991 and I wanted to be Chief Executive of an association. I was ambitious and wanted to run something myself and to grow it. Rather than be a director and stay at that level I thought that if I was going to progress in career terms I was going to have to make a shift. So I went to a smaller organisation. I was willing to sacrifice that scale to go to an organisation and try and build it up.

At Copec I was in a place that I knew really well which matched my own values, a concept called concomitance. When I first went to Parklands there was initially a mismatch. I worked to develop the association in a way that was closer to my values. I personally believed those values were the right ones and actually my values haven't shifted very much through my entire life.

On a Mission: Walsall Parklands

When I first joined what is now Accord over twenty years ago, Parklands had 460 units and about ten or eleven staff. We weren't doing very much at that stage. Parklands was quite small but within eighteen months we had persuaded Walsall and District Housing Association to join us. We grew through that and we managed to develop more by getting more money as a result of that merger.

By this time, the Conservative Government under Margaret Thatcher had adopted housing associations. They were organisations that were outside the Public Sector Borrowing Requirement (PSBR) and because of that they were funded by the Conservatives where they wouldn't fund councils. Ideologically, they wanted the size of the state to shrink; housing associations were an alternative to council housing and were seen as a permitted area of investment. We had austerity then. It was all about controlling the deficit and the debt in Thatcher's era and because housing associations were outside the PSBR we grew.

Some councils fell out with housing associations back then because they felt it was unfair. Housing associations were allowed to build and develop and have the money whilst local authorities were given very little. The Government also wanted to transfer councils' housing stock into housing associations or newly-set up housing associations. What they wanted to do was to privatise as much of the state as they could. It was going on in health, it was going on in education and a really big trend was going on in housing.

Interestingly the recent case law shows now that housing associations are seen as public authorities for much of what we do. Housing associations are now enmeshed and embodied in the state; so Thatcher's idea of privatisation has come full circle. We are regarded as so much part of the public sector, that we are seen as public sector agencies, which is the opposite to what she was trying to create.

Anyway I wanted Parklands to really meet housing needs in the way that I believed housing associations should meet such needs. I managed to form alliances with people on the Board such as Betty Deakin, Cheryl Kahn and Maurice Wolverson all of whom had got real commitment and shared that ethos, and so we transformed the mission and intent behind the organisation. We shifted from just providing housing to meeting real housing need – housing people on the local authority waiting list, building a relationship with the local authority, and meeting the needs of homeless people.

Walsall and District probably had a Christian basis when it was formed. A group of local committed people came together to try and meet housing need. They had that same mission that I always felt was important, although I am not a Christian; for me it was about being a force for good. So Walsall and District joined us and that reinforced the mission. It gave further drive at board level.

Betty Deakin was the Chair of Walsall and District and she was also involved in the Council of Voluntary Services and Chair of Age Concern in Walsall – so she had this ethos of doing good for people and wanting to change people's lives for the good. She brought an extra dimension to us and there were also a couple of vicars on the Walsall and District Board with strong values. Together they and Betty reinforced the drive for the merged association and the mission in a way in which we all believed.

We were also getting money from the Housing Corporation to grow. We merged – so that created scale; and we were building at a bigger scale than we had ever done before – so we were beginning to get momentum. We formed the Black Country Housing Association Group. I always felt that Birmingham had a bigger share of the cake than the Black Country so I tried to get together a group of organisations that worked in the Black Country to push for more resources for the area. That's what we did. I stood up at conferences and meetings and argued for the Black Country.

A Bigger Scale: Walsall Parkland and Westland to Accord

The Housing Corporation liked the Black Country Housing Association Group because in its view, the Birmingham lobby was too strong. We successfully attracted more resources for the Black Country. This helped us build at a greater scale as were other housing associations in the region. One of them was Westland Homes, which was also in the Black Country alliance that we had formed.

I never approached them but after a little while Gerry Cornell, the Chief Executive, came to me and said, 'I wonder if there is any scope in us working together and doing even more'. They worked in a different part of the Black Country to us. We were primarily Walsall; whilst they were based in Halesowen but were primarily Dudley, Sandwell and Wolverhampton –

Cutting the cake to celebrate the merger of Parklands and Westland Homes to create Accord in 1992. Holding the knife is Phil Wood, chair of Walsall Parklands and Betty Deakin, Chair of Walsall and District and Chief Executive of Walsall Council for Voluntary Service. On the left is Sid Wright, a Walsall councillor, and next to him is Jim Cornell, board member of Walsall and District, who was also the first chair of Caldmore Housing.

Between Betty and Phil is David Brown, an industrialist and chief executive of Jebron Limited. The lady on the right is Mary McNulty, a Walsall councillor, and next to her is Geoff Pearson, who had been involved with Walsall's Housing Department. Behind them on the left is Ken Buckler, also of Walsall CVS and on the right is Ken Draper, also from Walsall and District and Walsall Primary Care Trust.

where they had absorbed other housing associations a few years before which had two or three schemes.

Following discussions we got our respective Chairs talking and we decided to merge in 1992. I became the boss of the new organisation that we called Accord, but Gerry was very important. He was incredibly committed to housing, it was his life and soul. Gerry was a driving force behind Westland and a really important figure in bringing Accord together in those early stages as a bigger, scaled-up Black Country-wide organisation.

The Chairman of Parklands was Maurice Wolverson. He was a Douglas Hurd-type figure. A chartered accountant, he was Chair of the family

A photograph celebrating Accord Housing Association's involvement with Tipton City Challenge in 1993. On the right is Maurice Wolverson, chair of Accord, and behind him is Ken Draper.

practitioners' committee locally and the Chair of the health authority for Walsall. He was a public figure and we were lucky to get him. He was an establishment figure but he cared about people. Maurice was an important transitional figure as we turned into an organisation that was actually doing things for the community, meeting housing need in a significant way, and with Maurice we were showing we had credibility.

As for Westland, the chair was a physicist, Dr John Griffith, and the two of them got on well. When organisations come together it's always about people. I had established a good relationship with Gerry Cornell, their chief executive. We felt it was a good idea about coming together, our values were similar and we thought we could achieve more jointly and we thought we could build more homes – because it was all about meeting housing needs, remember, as there was a big waiting list then.

It was a similar situation to now – there was a massive housing crisis and councils were not allowed to build by the government. We could do more and we thought we ought to squeeze our assets and do more in order to meet that growing housing need out there.

We were the bigger organisation than Westland but we decided to transfer engagements, as we call it, to show them that we were genuine. A deal was struck between the Chairs and Boards that Maurice Wolverson would be chair of the new organisation for the first year and then John Griffith would become Chair. These mergers brought together greater resources both in terms of assets and people and it was a very exciting time.

Tenant Involvement: Birmingham Co-operative Housing Services

In this 1992 to 1996 period we really grew and from the start when we formed Accord we've always had a high level of tenant involvement. Tenants have been involved with our Board so that they would be party to the decision making; tenants have been involved in how we've been run for a long time; and tenants have always had a voice in our governance and our management.

Connie Dutton, who lived in one of our schemes in The Chuckery in Walsall, was an early tenant on our board and she was terrific. The contribution she made was important – plus she always used to bring in cakes to every board meeting – she was a fantastic cook. Connie was an important figure through her commitment and her humanity, and she'd got her feet on the ground.

Connie would always remind us about what was important for tenants and having that strong voice there, willing to speak up and working in a constructive way with other people, was important. She never felt 'oh there's an accountant speaking over here, that lawyer is speaking over there' – she never had a lesser voice. She brought that strength on behalf of the tenants and represented them really well.

Birmingham Co-operative Housing Services (bchs), joining us was very important for tenant leadership and tenant control. In 1992 there was a whole range of secondary co-ops in the UK, primarily in the big urban centres like Liverpool, Glasgow, London, and Birmingham. Most of them were struggling because the grant regime had changed. You now had to raise private finance in order to supplement the cost of schemes.

We used to get a 100% grant, so if you built a house the whole of that cost would be met by grant. We would even get a revenue deficit grant if we made a loss. If you ran a big deficit that showed you were meeting real need.

But when Thatcher and the Tories came into power what they wanted to do was have a mixed finance regime. So instead of having a 100% grant you would have, say, a 60% grant, then have to raise the rest of it from private finance and have a slightly higher rent to meet that cost. That mixed funding regime came into play and we were actually good at raising that money and we did well. We raised quite a lot of money early on and that changed the game entirely.

It was a period of radical and fundamental change and housing associations were able to borrow from the private sector but the co-ops couldn't. They were small organisations; the banks didn't like them and even if they could borrow money it would have been at actually quite high interest rates – whereas interest rates for us were very low. So the co-ops were frozen out of the development regime.

Secondary co-ops provided services to the primary co-ops. For example, two primary co-ops in Birmingham were Victoria and Triangle, whilst Paddock in Walsall was another example. They owned their stock and managed them themselves but bchs used to provide services to help them develop new schemes and also provide them with some professional management support if they needed it. Hence the secondary co-ops were backing up the primaries.

Because of that process and the lack of development income, those secondaries were struggling. The work wasn't there for them to survive. Some of them died but a number of them were absorbed into other housing associations, so bchs was looking for a partner. We worked with Paddock Housing Co-operative in Walsall and they suggested to bchs that they might want to join us. They had a competition and I had to go and give a presentation to their board and all of their members in Birmingham, as did other organisations. Copec was the main alternative and was a much bigger organisation than us but they went with us.

So bchs joined us in 1993 and we've really pushed tenant leadership ever since. It fits with our principles really well. The thing to do with power is to give it away. It's not to retain it, it's not to tell people what to do, it's not to be authoritarian – it's to actually help people, facilitate people to do things for themselves if they want. Hand power over and help them exercise decisions in their own communities.

We supported about fifteen co-ops at that time through bchs, which was also helping lots of tenant management organisations in local authority stock. Through that, at one stage we were supporting about 25,000 people. Tenant management became a really strong pillar in the Accord approach – encouraging people to take control of their own communities.

I think that is true of Caldmore as well, right from its start with the Action Group. They decided not to go along with what the Council wanted to do in demolishing houses in their community and instead fought it because of their belief in their community. This was true of Starley Housing Co-operative in Coventry too – they fought the Council to prevent the clearance of their homes and the loss of their community.

Chris Handy helping to lay the first bricks of the homes at Paddock Co-operative.

Certainly my view is this – let's help people to run their own communities and do things themselves. I think that approach satisfies two political opinions. On the right of the political spectrum you've got beliefs in Samuel Smiles and 'Self Help', so the Tories quite like it that people are doing these kinds of things; it's very Big Society. And on the left side of it, it's pure democracy; the people are in charge, they're deciding things for themselves and they're running things for themselves. Ever since 1992 that's been a key feature of the Accord way of doing things.

Exciting Times: Growing Accord

The excitement of that period in the 1990s drove us on. In organisations as they get bigger, you get growing pains and you have to tackle certain things and do things in new ways. Originally when Parklands and Westland joined forces we used to have separate teams at certain levels and it was clear after a while that this approach wasn't really working. So part of the growing pains was about bringing teams together so that it was group-wide rather than simply the same organisations in the same place but doing things separately. We still do things differently sometimes due to context.

Back then we were building on a scale that we had never done before. That was what was driving the organisation – to meet the housing crisis needs. We were doing that and it was very satisfying, giving the keys to somebody and to open a scheme over here or there. You were providing people with stable homes which is the foundation of a good life – not on its own, but it's a good start, and that really drove us all on.

When I joined Parklands we had 463 units, then it was about 1,100 units when Walsall and District joined us. Westland had about 700 and bchs had about 700 – so it was about 2,500 when we all joined up. Now we have 11,000 properties, we've got 1,700 staff and, if you include development, we have a turnover of well over £100 million a year. Lots of people contributed to that journey, to growing to that scale, people who have played a really important part in getting us to where we are now.

We do much more now than we've ever done. We now let something like 700 homes a year – we didn't even have that number when I first joined. That's the kind of scale we're dealing with. We're building about 400 homes a year and the others are re-lets of properties that become empty. We've got a development programme of over 2,000 units over the next three years. We're still building, we're still using all of those assets to build more and provide homes for people in need but we are doing lots of other things now.

Chris Handy, chief executive of Accord Housing Association shaking hands with Mrs June Millington, head teacher at Park Lane Infant School, Sedgley. The occasion was a sod-cutting ceremony locally in 1994.

Up until the late 1990s we were still getting grant levels of probably 60% and just raising small amounts of private finance to make the schemes work. Since then the level of grant per scheme has eroded through value for money efficiency initiatives or whatever. We are now down, probably, to a 20% grant for the total cost of a home. That means that 80% of the money now is coming from the private sector, from bank loans.

Care and Support from Accord

As well as housing, what we've also been doing since at least the mid-1990s is to provide care and support for people. Providing a home is a good foundation for a settled way of life but it's not enough on its own. By providing care and support for people, we can help them to sustain their tenancies and live independent lives within the community.

Our care and support operation has grown. Initially we had probably half a dozen schemes with people like Mencap, Mind and so on that we used to support. We ran some schemes ourselves, particularly for older people. But providing care for people and diversifying our activities became a bigger and bigger part of our business. Providing care and support for older people is a key specialism.

We also have expertise within the organisation around dementia and we've got eighteen schemes of extra care for older people right across the Midlands – from Solihull to Telford. There are eight in Walsall on its own, and we've just built a fantastic scheme over in Bushbury in Wolverhampton. About a third of our residents are older people. Some of those are in specialist schemes and some are living independently in their own homes. We've also got a domiciliary care service and we're hoping to expand that because often people don't want to go into institutions; they want to live in their own home.

Sixty million of our turnover, over half of our business, is in care and support for people. We also support people with learning disabilities; young single and homeless; women and children suffering domestic violence, and that has been an important aspect of our work; people with mental health needs; and people with substance addiction, whether it be alcohol or drugs. We support almost all of the areas of specialist needs.

Miss Betty Boothroyd MP, now Baroness Boothroyd of Sandwell, opening Exon Court, a sheltered scheme in Tipton, on 27 September 1989.

MP Dave Wright visits Millbrook Day Centre with our former Director of Care and Support, Maureen Bradley.

Seventy-five per cent of our 11,000 tenants, some of whom are older people, are on benefit directly. So we get the rent paid to us on their behalf. That means that many of them are out of work. It's a very big proportion of our tenants and that has grown during the recession. Over the last three years that figure has risen.

In the main the people that we house are in the lower socio-economic groups. They are not skilled or are semi-skilled – or else they worked in industrial sectors in the Black Country that have declined and so there aren't jobs out there for them now. Even if they are skilled, they've got the wrong skills to match the job market. This means that our tenants are disproportionately affected by recession; they've been in marginal employment and have lost their jobs first.

LoCaL Homes from Accord

The fact that many of our tenants are out of work has had a big impact. The Group is trying to create training opportunities, job opportunities and also enterprise opportunities to create pathways into work. A good example of that is LoCaL Homes. We've had an initiative with a Norwegian company called Hedalm Anebyhus for about seven or eight years. It's a co-operative and they manufacture modular homes in a factory.

They are really good quality and super insulated as they have to cope with the low temperatures in Norway; they are wooden homes but they're not log cabins as they are much better than that. We've been importing these and putting them up in Redditch, and a place there that they call 'Little Norway' was the first scheme. People love them as they're more spacious than the homes we traditionally build over here.

We've agreed with the Norwegian company that we will build the homes here in the UK. Walsall Council has worked with us in a partnership on this initiative and has provided us with a building and some money. We've now got a factory in Walsall that is producing up to 200 homes a year and employs 30 people – and they're either tenants of ours or they're people from that local community. That's quite a big initiative because it's a big turnover and we are trying to create a number of initiatives like that where we create opportunities for people to work. I would personally like to see more of our tenants working directly for the Group and with LoCaL Homes.

There are many examples where people get involved through their communities, get skilled up, gain confidence and self-esteem – and all that

Accord's factory LoCaL Homes.

has enabled them to go on training courses and get jobs. Education in a traditional sense may not have been very good for them, but because now they've had a different kind of learning and training that's been fixed around them then they've really taken off as individuals. You can really transform people's lives.

AddVentures from Accord

Another great initiative we've got going at the moment is called *AddVentures*. It's based upon the Tides Foundation in America. To use the American language, it's called a fiscal sponsorship initiative. It's a charity that enables people to set up a project to help with a particular good cause. To do so in this country you have to set up a charity and you spend so much energy trying to set it up that you are worn out by the time you get it going. But what you can

do with this American model is to set up the project and then use the charitable shield status of the organisation. You get going immediately and all the back office service is provided to you.

We've set that up here with Add-Ventures and we are sponsoring two types of organisations. First, and under the charitable umbrella of Accord, we are setting up initiatives like *Planning for Real, LoCaL Homes, Greenscape* and others that are employment-based projects. They can either stay in the Group, or if they are successful, they can come out and be an enterprise in their own right. That means we incubate projects, we start them off and create jobs. Greenscape, for example, which is a grounds maintenance and cleaning company, employs well over 50 people and a number of them are tenants.

The second strand to AddVentures is that we are trying to encourage tenants to set up their own businesses. We've got 22 of those going through and we've been running road shows to bring tenants in to see what ideas and dreams they've got.

Chris Handy, chief executive of Accord Housing, flanked by staff members Caroline Coulman, left, and Debbie Morris celebrating the fortieth anniversary of the housing association in May 2005; thanks to the Express and Star. *The anniversary related to the founding of Westland Homes in May 1965.*

What we have done to achieve this is to reconfigure the service we provide. We have trained up a whole series of front-line workers to help tenants to realise their aspirations around businesses. So we have twelve trained people to give business support to start-ups. They are the champions, who mentor, coach and support the AddVenturers, the people actually starting up the businesses, so that they can thrive. We also buy their work from them; so we use our purchasing power to help sustain them in the early stages – and we'll do much more of that going forward. We are trying to help people but we are not telling them they have got to do this.

Part of this approach is the old Rubery Owen building in Darlaston, which is an incubator unit for start-up businesses. David Owen is a fantastic man and he gave us this building of over 20,000 square feet because he wants to leave a legacy locally. Rubery Owen was a very important business for Darlaston and the Midlands. David wanted to donate the building so that small businesses could thrive, and so much does he believe in the project that he has kept his offices there and he gives us £25,000 a year in

Chris Handy, Chief Executive of the Accord Group with Shadow Housing Minister Jack Dromey MP and MP for Walsall South, Valerie Vaz having a tour of a brand new £10 million development of 90 low carbon timber frame homes.

rent as a contribution to making this whole initiative work. We call it Rubery Owen Innovation Works so we don't lose the Rubery Owen link and we have a number of small businesses operating there.

Today we are giving a much wider offer. There's housing but also there's this contribution to local communities in a much more significant way. However, looking back we have built a lot of homes for people that have needed them and we must not underestimate the contribution that this makes to people's lives.

Having a stable home is the basis of having a potentially thriving life and unless you've got that it is very hard. If you're homeless you're more likely to be attacked and you're more likely to have a whole range of infectious diseases. It's that physical reality. If you've got shelter and it's of decent quality then you have the foundation for a good life.

So providing housing is a major thing that we have done as an organisation. In addition to that, the care and support we have provided has been terrific. We have supported people to live independent lives, quality lives, the lives that they want to lead in the community. Now looking forward we've got those firm foundations so we can help people get into work.

Chapter 3

MORE THAN A LANDLORD: WALSALL PARKLANDS TO ACCORD

Wendy Powell, Director for Transformation

Resident Led

I grew up in Darlaston and Bentley and then went to university at Bath to study for a degree in Home Economics as I was interested in food science and nutrition. Then in the last year of my degree in 1981 we focused on social welfare and the history of housing. That year I did my last dissertation around Bournville Village Trust and about getting communities involved in play and activities for young people.

I did quite a lot of the research in Birmingham and that triggered off my initial interest in housing. That was because Bournville Village Trust didn't do just housing as they did a lot of charitable work and work for the community. It was very much a community-focused organisation and still is today.

Then the first job I had was as a housing assistant with Wolverhampton Council. It was working with the rents and voids team, and at that time it was when people would go out to collect the rents by knocking doors. But my job didn't really involve people, it was just dealing with the processes – when a property became empty, re-letting it to someone else. After about eighteen months I was employed by Parklands Housing Society in Walsall as a housing assistant. Becoming involved with Parklands was very different. It involved meeting people and it was customer focused.

I joined Parklands in 1982, so this year I will have been 30 years with this organisation that has changed so much, beyond belief over that time. Then it was very small, led by a board of volunteer members. It had originated from Parklands Gardens, off the Birmingham Road. This was property in which board members had been involved in as shareholders and with which they were interested in the management.

Parklands Housing Society developed from this in the 1960s. At that time they weren't building any new properties. They had just about got their first lot of grants from the Housing Corporation and in the 1970s they had built properties up at King's Hill in Darlaston, which are the oldest ones that we manage now. They also had property in Tipton and Wolverhampton, so they had started to spread a little bit outside Walsall but Darlaston and the centre of Walsall was their main focus.

We also had a little office in Lower Hall Lane, an old property that Age UK now use as their offices. We had to move out as we grew. In terms of staff, there were probably only about ten of us maximum, and that included a couple of rent collectors. There was me as the housing assistant, the housing manager and then the chief executive, who was called the director, who was only part-time.

He was Desmond Harrison of Fox and Harrison, the estate agents and valuers. Fox and Harrison worked in Lower Hall Lane and we were based in their offices. So the Housing Society came out of estate agency and property

Looking down from St Matthew's, the parish church of Walsall, to one of the oldest parts of Walsall – The Ditch; thanks to the Express and Star. This photograph was taken in 1970, soon before The Ditch disappeared. In the background are the multi-story blocks of flats of The Paddock – and area where the Paddock Housing Co-operative would later emerge; it is now part of the Accord Group.

management. He was involved in property sales but he had a charitable interest: 'what else can we do for people that can't afford to buy a property' was what he asked. He believed that he could do more and I think the board of voluntary members at the time were exactly the same. They were all homeowners but they could see that there was a need in Walsall for people who couldn't aspire to that.

My role as housing assistant involved everything from managing and maintaining the waiting list for people who were interested in being rehoused; working with the local authority, as it still owned and managed its own housing; making sure people paid their rent on time and helping them if they couldn't; and dealing with anti-social behaviour, the same as we do today. But it was all on a very much more local scale.

One of the biggest things we did then, which was quite novel, was we had a big 'Tenants' Liaison Committee' as we called it. This involved representatives from the various schemes that we had coming together to talk about how they

The mayor of Walsall, Councillor Harry Ashby, opening the first phase of 159 homes to be developed at King's Hill, Darlaston in June 1975; thanks to the Express and Star. On the left is Phil Wood, chair of Parklands. The homes were part of a £240,000 scheme by the Parklands Housing Association and were all let to people on either the Association's own waiting list or to those nominated from the council's waiting list. King's Hill is the most sustainable scheme in the Accord Group.

could improve things and what issues they could deal with. It was very much resident led at that time, which is the same approach today – but then it was much more novel.

One of the original chairs of that committee was Charles Holland, who lived at King's Hill. He was very interested in improving the estate and making sure it was looked after. Charles sat on the board. There was representation at board level from residents and there always has been, but it was unusual all those years ago.

When I joined Parklands, we also had responsibility for managing some properties on behalf of the trustees of alms houses. We've gathered some more over time. They are mainly in Walsall and include Crump's Alms Houses and the Henry Boys Alms Houses. We've now got trustees on all of those charities and we service the board of each charity by providing management support, secretarial support, taking the minutes and other things.

Crump's was small but it did do some development through Accord and built some more properties, but there are others that had a board of trustees to manage just two or three properties. Through the Almshouse Association, we persuaded these tiny charities to come together as one – with local councillors and representation from Accord and us managing them; although Henry Boys is still separate as they have more properties.

We do the general management of the properties, we let them, we advertise any vacancies, look after the finances, and make the official returns. So there is back office support and management on a day-to-day basis like collecting the fees to live there. The fees used to be very tiny and we had to explain to the trustees about getting more income from the properties to keep them up whilst still keeping the fees fair and affordable.

We've tried to keep to the criteria set up when the charities were started, but sometimes we've had to go to the Almshouse Association and ask them if the terms of bequest could be altered as the criteria were so difficult to meet in the twentieth century let alone the twenty-first century.

Rapid Development: the 1980s and 1990s

Parklands developed quite rapidly in the 1980s and 90s. The organisation became bigger. We moved from the small offices in Lower Hall Lane to bigger offices in Hatherton Street and we joined up with Walsall and District Housing Trust. That had been based in a property on the Birmingham Road. Again it was very small and very similar in size to Parklands.

Walsall and District was an organisation of about half a dozen people who did similar work in Walsall with schemes in Leamore and Bloxwich.

Interestingly they'd also got a scheme in Cannock, as did Parklands. I believe that they also started from estate agents, in their case A. J. Llewellyn estate agents, and they were also socially concerned.

The approach was made for Parklands and Walsall and District to get together and do more things together. So we joined up. Their offices in Birmingham Road were closed and their staff moved in with us in Hatherton Street. We then became Walsall Parklands. Their housing officers joined with our housing officers and we became a more professional service.

Then we joined with Westland Homes in 1992 and became Accord. We retained their offices in Halesowen for a while as we still had stock in

On the left is David Brown, deputy chair of Accord Group, and to the right is the mayor of Walsall's consort, Doreen Farrell. The next lady is Mary McNulty and with his back to the camera is the mayor of Walsall Council Councillor Ray Farrell. This photo was taken in 1992 in Castle Street, which was part of the Booth Street scheme of former Rubery Owen houses.

Halesowen and properties in the Dudley area, and we had to think carefully about how customers were going to access us. But the Halesowen offices themselves weren't particularly accessible on the top floor of an office block. After consulting with the customers, the decision was made to close them.

We then moved to new premises in West Bromwich. The building was only three stories high but as we have expanded another floor has gone on. That became the central services offices, where the corporate teams are. We also had a shop in Tipton in the town centre as we had stock there, but we closed it as there weren't that many properties in the area to make it viable and there wasn't much footfall in the shop.

Not long after we joined with Westland, Birmingham Co-operative Housing Services joined us and so quickly in the 1990s the structure of the organisation changed because all of those organisations were very different. They'd all got that local flavour, that particular type of service or housing; so bchs was very different, working with co-operatives for instance, to what we had been doing as Westland and Walsall Parklands.

During this time we started to get quite a lot of grants from the Housing Corporation to develop new schemes. We probably had our biggest boom in building then. I remember us handing over one scheme in Darlaston and one in Pelsall and altogether we had about 150 properties in one handover in one week. We had no problem in letting them at all because there was always a huge demand for them.

We now also had a bigger development team. In the early 80s we just had the development director and an assistant but we had to employ more people as we were working with partners, architects and others. So the development team had a bigger responsibility and we also started to do sales of housing through shared ownership.

Then we acquired the present Accord offices in Darlaston in the 90s. It was on a small scale at first but then we grew so that we now occupy two old buildings. The first part we took over used to be a sweet shop, with flats above it that we rented out. We had an office downstairs with just three staff in. Then we expanded and we needed upstairs. We rehoused the people in the flats and turned them into offices.

We expanded again and we acquired the old 'White Lion' pub next door when it became empty. We converted that into offices downstairs and flats above, and eventually they were converted into office space and we filled it up. There are 30 people working here now whereas there were three to start with.

Initially we moved here because of the location of our properties. Our local housing stock is managed from here and the offices are accessible to

Renovation of workers homes in Darlaston previously owned by Rubery Owen.

the people because they can walk here. The other office that we have in Caldmore is for the people in our properties in central Walsall.

The 1980s and 1990s were a great learning curve. We went from secure tenancies to assured tenancies, so there was a big change in the terms of the legality of the tenancy agreements we had and of the rights of tenants because of the 1988 Housing Act. Secure tenants had the right to buy, assured tenants didn't. The legislation became more complex.

Everything became computerised as well; when I started everything had been paper based. We had on file all the letters that we wrote to people but now it is all electronic. Rent collecting was changed – people could pay using cards or by coming into the office. You didn't need people knocking doors, although looking at rent arrears now I think people knocking doors, which is what our community housing officers do, is still the most effective way of having a conversation with somebody who is in difficulty.

Everything was technologically improved, systems changed and it became a big organisation – but we had to make sure to involve tenants so that we didn't lose that community feeling. We didn't want to get bigger and bigger and bigger and for residents to feel that they had no relationship with us, that

Typical renovation of older houses by Accord in the 1990s – in this case in Darlaston.

they just paid the rent and we were their landlord and that was it. We had to make sure we held on to tenant involvement amidst those changes.

We kept that tenants' liaison committee going and it still exists today in another guise. We have had to create committees for various areas. There are still only a small number of people who want to get involved but they think it is a good thing to get involved because they have a say in how things are managed. And with the Queen's Diamond Jubilee a lot more people have become involved.

When I first joined we had quite small waiting lists but that became bigger and bigger, particularly for houses. We never had any difficulty in letting any of our apartments or flats. Today people have choice. There are choice-based lettings schemes, but back then we kept area-based waiting lists. As soon as we had a property that became available we never had any difficulty in letting it.

The criteria for people becoming tenants were very similar to what they are now: the threat of homelessness or homelessness. Maybe they'd got a property of their own where they were struggling to pay the mortgage or had lost a job or whatever. These things are the same now as they were in the 80s. They would be a priority. People suffering domestic violence, particularly women – they would be a priority to be moved, as would people who had any other threat to their lives or their family. Things like people moving to the area for work, leaving the armed forces are also priorities. Then there are people from family homes, older children needing to leave home for their independence.

When I first started at Parklands we probably only had about a thousand properties at the most. By the end of the 90s that had probably quadrupled. The growth was quick over that ten-year period and now we've got up to 11,000 properties. And so more staff had to be employed and they had to be trained.

When I got into housing, most people I know who worked in housing at that time came into housing by accident. It was an interesting job, but the

On 18 September 1986 Princess Anne opened Old Vicarage Close in Pelsall. Behind her is Councillor Phil Wood, chairman of the Parklands Housing Society. The scheme consisted of two blocks of flats and bungalows for older people, all of whom were covered by a twenty-four hour warden service in case of an emergency.

Chartered Institute of Housing professionalised things because you could do training through them and there were lots of other training agencies. So today people have a range of training and professional qualifications that relate specifically to housing. None of these existed then, it was more general knowledge, a bit of common sense and learning on the job.

When I joined we had done general housing and didn't do anything else, but then we started to do supported housing for people who had extra care and support needs. Until the early 90s we hadn't done anything other than the sheltered housing for older people, where there was the traditional warden on site in case they had any needs during the day and who checked on them and was on call should they need help. That was the only kind of supported housing we did.

Then during the 1990s we did a lot of work with customers who had mental health concerns and with people with learning disabilities. We worked with other agencies like Mencap in projects. We were the owners of the buildings but they, being the experts in that service, managed and ran that service.

So we started to work with a lot more external agencies as partners. They could deliver certain things better than us but we could do the housing, although now we have a lot of other expertise in-house. We have whole care and support teams across the Group that have a specialism, although they still work with partners. I think, though, during the 90s there was a recognition that people had particular needs. Not everybody is the same and we shouldn't be treating them the same and offering the same service to everyone.

Working with People

People like that personal service; people are individuals and they've all got different needs at different times of their lives. What we want to do is offer a service to somebody whatever it is that they and their family need. And those needs might change while they're tenants of ours. They might be single or a couple, and then have kids and maybe the kids leave and they become older and they need more support services.

What we are doing is trying to hold on to them as customers as their needs change. Maybe when they become older, moving them to a property that is more suitable, like a bungalow, or offering a service with support.

We've recently had a restructuring of our team so that what were our two offices in Darlaston and Caldmore we are calling a locality team. They focus on that locality where we have properties but also on the residents and the communities around where we have properties. We can work in that area for the benefit of all of the people, not just our customers. So we work with local schools, where our tenants' children might go, to see what we can do there to encourage those kids to manage their money when they're older, what to do when they come to look for property.

I started with the Group as housing assistant then became housing manager because the previous person was on maternity leave. It was a temporary move but then she decided not to come back. Then as we expanded I became a director and it became more professional with a full-time chief executive in Chris Handy, with all his experience and his vision for what the organisation could look like in terms of growth and all those other things we could do. He is very ambitious about all those things, not just about housing but about digital inclusion and youth engagement – and we are all behind him in doing that.

Now my job's changed. We are working very closely with the two locality teams that are doing the housing, but they and us together are looking at things that we can do outside housing: the jobs and skills, the training and vocational opportunities for customers.

The Accord Group offices in the old 'White Lion' in Darlaston.

Darlaston and Caldmore have high youth unemployment and a high poverty profile. I've seen how Darlaston has lost its way a little bit. The town centre, in particular, needs regenerating and I think Accord can be here to help. We're members of the town centre partnership, for instance, and it's great to be part of that as I am from here.

We work in areas where poverty, unemployment, and the needs of young people out of work are the highest so we can't just sit back and say we're just a landlord, we're not concerned for you and your family. We are trying to find out more about our customers so that we know what their needs are as individuals and families so that we can offer those extra things that they might want from us.

It's a bit of a culture change for them and us. We are not just your landlord, we'd like to do this – therefore we've got to make sure that our customers know that we can do these extra things. It's definitely becoming a more personalised service. We want to enable our customers to become independent and not reliant on us.

We're not going to do things for them, we want to encourage them to do things for themselves. We want to get them from wherever they are now and on that journey to doing everything for themselves and getting them involved and confident – and able to go out there and look for work. So some of our work will be around helping them write a CV or a personal statement – or whatever it is they need. It might be working with a younger person or an older person that's lost a job. The whole ethos of the organisation is working with people and not for them. It goes back to the old tenants' liaison committee and to residents' engagement. Engage with them to enable them to decide what they want us to do.

We need to make sure we are very professional, that we are meeting the highest standards we can, that we keep that local community feeling, and that we make sure our teams are out there talking to customers about what they want from us and what we can do better. We must make sure we are accessible, always welcome customers' views and get them involved in the services we provide.

Walsall and District Housing Trust to Accord
Ken Draper

My initial link with housing associations was when I was asked to be a member of the Board of Walsall Housing Trust chaired by Miss Betty Deakin. At that time I was the general administrator with Walsall Heath Authority. The policy of the Housing Corporation had changed and small housing associations were not considered to be viable and plans of amalgamation were introduced. As a result Walsall Housing Trust was merged with Parklands Housing Association and I became a member of the Board of Management.

The Housing Corporation continued with its amalgamation policy and Parklands became merged with the newly formed Accord Housing Association. I became a member of Accord's Board of Management and was for some time chairman of its Personnel Committee.

Accord has grown tremendously over the years and must be one of the most respected Housing Groups in the country, being very ably led by Dr Christopher Handy.

In my opinion, the essential difference between the old local authority estates and Accord schemes has been the variety of housing designs and housing schemes and the introduction of shared ownership. The jewel in the crown for Walsall was the conversion of the old school in Tantarra Street into a very successful warden controlled residential housing for the elderly.

Chapter 4

DOING SOMETHING ABOUT HOUSING: WESTLAND HOMES TO ACCORD

Recollections of the Westland Years
John Griffith

Early in 1975 I was a lecturer in physics at the University of Birmingham, just returned from a year's sabbatical in Minnesota. Having dinner with Ken Maslen, then a senior partner at solicitors Edge and Ellison, I rashly asked, 'Why doesn't someone do something about the housing problem in this country?' To which he replied, 'How would you like to try?'

Ken was then chair of Westland Homes Housing Society, which had been formed to build co-ownership housing developments. It was run out of his office and the management comprised other professionals who did work for the Society. The 1974 Housing Act had just made substantial public funds available for housing associations to build houses for rent, but on condition that all professionals doing work on such projects left the management.

And so I found myself on a committee with several other interested folk, who mainly had in common an absence of knowledge of housing. A couple of years later I was the Chair, remaining in that post until the merger with Walsall Parklands in 1991 created Accord Housing, after which I alternated in the chair with Maurice Wolverson until I retired in 2001 having left the West Midlands.

At the time of my joining, Westland Homes had no staff, but was developing the large estate at Kitwell Lane, close to the M5 in Birmingham. Seeing that this had nearly 150 dwellings, we soon took on a General Manager (later Chief Executive), a Housing Officer, a secretary and a small office on the Hagley Road. Not long after this the Rowleys Green Lane development in Coventry was built along with other smaller sites and the Society had around 250 dwellings to manage.

It was a steep learning curve! In Coventry we thought it would be a smart idea to place the children's play area below the elderly persons' flats, so the residents could look out on the youngsters enjoying life. It took the senior citizens about three weeks to point out the error of our ways – forcefully. Kitwell Lane had an underground garage, which caused huge trouble by attracting most of the undesirables in west Birmingham and taxed our ingenuity for much of my remaining time as Chair. Steadily we learned to ask tenants what they wanted. It works better that way.

In 1982 we completed a development near the centre of Halesowen, whence we had moved our office as the staff numbers grew. It seemed a good idea to promote ourselves locally so we asked the local MP, then John Stokes, to open the development. Thus in May 1982 we assembled for the opening and were delighted to see the Press turn up in force. They were not in the least interested in housing, but only to question the MP on the liberation of the Falklands. It was my first public opening and I overheard someone from the Housing Corporation muttering, 'I didn't think they made chairmen that young'.

Westland Homes grew fairly quickly to about twenty staff and 700 plus dwellings. In the 1980s we branched out into privately funded sheltered elderly schemes. The theory was that people moving into them would leave family housing vacant and any profit made could cross-subsidise our public housing. The first two schemes worked very well; however, we were then faced

Building work for Westland Homes at Hamilton Avenue in Halesowen in 1983.

by the 1988 housing crash and rapidly discovered the perils of entering the commercial market.

The ensuing difficulties and the attention they brought from the Housing Corporation began to threaten the Society, but it was also difficult for a smaller association to cope with development in the funding regime which was coming in. Initially the Government had funded Housing Association projects by large capital grants, which made low rents feasible. The switch was later made to private finance supported by commercial rents, which the Government funded through Housing Benefit. This regime favoured larger associations and was eventually the trigger which caused us to seek a merger and led to our marriage with Walsall Parklands to form Accord Housing.

It is good to look back on those interesting years in housing – so different from my day-job, to reflect on the success of Accord Housing and to realise that the country still has a housing problem. Would anyone like to try to do something about it?

Massive Changes
Sally McCready, Business Support Manager

I was at college doing a general reception course in 1981/82 and I needed a placement for a month as part of my college work. I found one with what was Westland Homes in Halesowen. I went there for a month just helping out. It was more to do with reception and I didn't really learn a lot about housing in that time. That was March and then in April they rang me up and asked me if I wanted a job as an office junior because that position had become available. I started on 24 May.

Westland's then was extremely small with about ten members of staff and we had probably a few hundred units, houses and flats, mainly for general needs. Local authorities used to send customers to us who had gone to them and if they weren't homeless or in dire need they were told that there were alternatives. So we would get customers come through the door that weren't eligible for local authority housing but were eligible for us.

We had quite a few schemes but centred around Halesowen and in to Birmingham, and we did have a big scheme in Coventry of about 140 units that was the furthest away. On top of that we had old co-ownership housing, where normally people rented an apartment and they paid a higher rent so that at a period in the future they could buy those apartments with a discount on the rent that they had paid.

We had two housing officers who had a generic housing role. They did everything from lettings through housing management to evictions, if there were any. We also did right-to-buy sales, so existing customers could buy their properties if they wanted to. Everything was done manually. We had no computers, so we had two people in finance who would deal with all the book work but also everybody's rent account.

We had a chief executive, a clerk of works and an assistant director, who used to oversee day-to-day things and policies and procedures. But in those days our policies and procedures were very vague, they might have been a page long. As an office junior I didn't get involved in the housing side as such. I would take a phone call and pass it on to the housing officer. You didn't need that level of information; you worked for a housing association, a housing society as it was then, and all you did was field the calls to the appropriate people. As long as you were seen as a junior member of staff you didn't need to know what was going on.

You were there to do the menial duties. Thirty years ago that was like a lot of organisations, if you were an office junior you did what you were told. You weren't allowed a lot of initiative. Policies and processes were dealt with

Building ten flats for Westland Homes for the over-55s in Wrights Lane, Old Hill in 1983.

by those people above you from housing officer upwards to the chief executive – and then the board of managers that made the decisions.

Changes since then have been absolutely huge. Now we don't have office juniors, or lower staff that would do menial jobs because we all get involved with people. So now we have receptionists and they have all the training that's needed so that when a call comes in they can actually deal with those calls. They don't need to pass that call on unless they get to a level where there are so many calls coming in or they can't help they have to move some on. But they do have that knowledge to assist people.

It's more of a one-stop – if someone comes in or they're on the phone, you deal with them as best you can and if they need to be transferred then they are transferred. Everybody has the training on the policies, on the documentation and on what properties we've got. People are more knowledgeable.

We've seen a lot of changes with people coming in at an assistant level who actually move in through the system and can become housing officers and managers. Accord does have a good ethos with investing in its employees to train them and keep them within the company. But when I started as a junior I used to have to go and fetch the chief executive's lunch every day, which was two sausage rolls and an apple pie. I used to have to make coffee at certain times of the day, that was part of my role, and take the banking to the night safe at five o'clock at night. All of those things wouldn't happen now, and you wouldn't expect that now. I think the expectations of employers and employees have changed to what they were then.

I'd never heard of a housing association until I went to work there. My family owned their own property and I didn't know anything about rented accommodation until I went to work for Westland Homes. But the information that they gave you to start with was very vague. Then, as the years progressed, people generally, even outside an association, became much more aware there were more opportunities out there. I think it's more publicised than it was then.

It was probably about four years before we ever put a property out on the market to attract people into our properties. That was because it was a shared ownership property which was something that was unheard of back in about 1986. That was the first advert I'd seen go out from the company to attract new customers for a different type of property.

That scheme was Vicarage Close in Stourbridge and the same year Walsall Parklands did their first shared ownership scheme which was Park View in Darlaston. They were both for first-time buyers, who part-rented and part-bought the properties. Over time they could buy more shares, if their circumstances allowed them to.

They were for people whose combined incomes were below a certain amount, because if it was more it was deemed that they could go and buy elsewhere. In those days we sold those 25% shares for £4,000 and the rents were quite low. We had people queuing up for them as they were the first of their type within Dudley Borough. Then we had quite a programme for first-time buyer accommodation, mainly throughout Dudley and Sandwell.

In 1982 there was a merger or a takeover between Westland Homes and Churchwell Housing. Churchwell had probably the similar amount of properties but they were purely managed by a committee, there was only one housing person and a secretary. They merged to form Westland Homes Housing Society, a bigger organisation with one committee of management. That was when they moved to Halesowen.

In those days, the committees were there just to agree the principles, to look at the accounts and act as an approver. Now our boards of management are a lot more involved; they're not just there to rubber stamp things, whereas in those days they relied on the chief executive to complete all the processes. All the board members were voluntary. There was a building society manager, a solicitor, a surveyor, accountants, a vicar – all professional people but mostly semi-retired or retired.

So then after the merger, they'd got properties throughout Halesowen, some in Bartley Green in Birmingham, Coventry and a couple of schemes in Wolverhampton. But in total there were no more than 500 properties. But we still didn't have a lot to do with the management of the accommodation; it was down to the housing officer at the time, Norma.

She used to go to Coventry about two days a week. We also had a lady there who acted a bit like a caretaker, so she would have keys and would help deal with repairs. It was a large scheme of over 140 odd units over probably three or four roads and people would go to her and then she would contact us to deal with the repairs or the voids or any issues that were on site.

I think she was unpaid as well, so it was done as a favour. In those days you could do that. We would send her a bunch of flowers at different times, and she would perhaps come to the Christmas meal. There was no office in Coventry, so the housing officer had to work out of her car and so she had to make sure she had everything she needed to go out and work on that site.

The tenants didn't have a say at all. There was no consultation, it was 'we're doing this and that's that'. We did their repairs, we put their rents up. There were no tenants on the management committee. That's changed

The opening of Westland Homes Crauford Court in Old Winsford on 11 July 1985. On the left is Gerry Cornell, the chief executive of Westland Homes and between him and the dignitary unveiling the plaque is the chair John Griffith.

totally. We've been involved with tenant engagement for a number of years and they've actually got more say in what's going on. We've got tenants' representatives elected to sit on our committees. When we devise a new policy, it will go out to a tenants' group or a tenants' panel so that they can go through the policy and see what they think. Not only do we consult with the whole groups as customers we also consult with smaller groups about what we should be doing in particular.

Customers have a lot more involvement but I think there is still more to do in attracting some client groups onto residents' panels, like the elderly who may be more infirm and don't drive. For example, should we be giving them transport to get to meetings or holding meetings closer to them? I am sure there are lots of people who would want to be involved but they may be housebound. And we need to reach out more to the younger generation, eighteen to twenty-five year olds, and convince them of the reasons why they should be involved.

Over the last fifteen years and more I've worked predominantly with home owners and seen big changes there. They may have got into difficulties with their mortgages and gone into rented accommodation. I think housing associations are more widely broadcast and advertised and people have got more access to the internet so it's easier to look for housing now. The internet will bring up lots of organisations, so now instead of people going predominantly to the local authority they will start coming to housing associations and they have done for probably for the last fifteen to twenty years.

But those first ten years in the 1980s was extremely difficult. What did people do? If you couldn't buy or go to the local authority where did you go? The Government brought in the Right to Buy legislation and said 'Let's sell everything off but we won't replace it' – which is why, I think, housing associations became better known. It was the housing associations that could get a grant to build.

Putting the finishing touch to new houses Westland Homes in Love Lane, The Lye in the 1980s.

I think the social role of helping people is important and with the Localism Act that came in April 2012 it will be even more so. We've just reorganised with **Caldmore**accord and our housing officers now are becoming more like mini-social workers. They are going to be more involved with our customers, know more about how to help with the wants and needs of those customers – as opposed to being a landlord that collects their rent, does their repairs and evicts them if that's what needs to happen.

They are actually going to get to know customers better so as to help them. Can we get them into work? Is that accommodation right for you? Should you be in a different type of accommodation? They will know them more, perhaps on first name terms, which in some ways is how we were back in the early 80s. We'd got a lot less customers and we knew them and it was more of a personal touch. People would ring up and you'd got on to first name terms with them.

But it's down to the individual. I've got customers now that I've dealt with for probably twenty years and when you first meet them it's Mr and Mrs, but over a period of time they will say to you, the older generation, 'Oh call me Fred' or 'Call me whatever'. Sometimes I still find that uncomfortable, because my age group was brought up to call people Mr or Mrs, auntie or uncle even though they weren't relatives but close neighbours; whereas the younger generation probably find first name terms easier. It is to do with respecting your clients and experience.

We then merged with Walsall Parklands in 1992. The offices remained as they were. We had a Halesowen office and a Walsall office but the teams were amalgamated. So the finance team became one large team and by then even Westlands was computerised, although we shared the computers.

I think there were changes after the merger but they were more to do with policies and procedures. Westland had always worked in the ethos as long as you knew what your job was then there weren't many policies and procedures; whereas with Walsall Parklands there were a lot of policies and procedures and we learnt from them.

Walsall Parklands was more driven by that process whereas with Westland it was sort of 'if you get from A to B and it's okay and these are the rules that you don't break then that's what you did'. Apart from somebody's tenancy agreement, which you had to follow, with the staff element you knew what to follow but it wasn't really written down.

That was a big change for Westland, in that people had to start following correct processes. Then they closed the Halesowen office and we moved to West Bromwich. They moved the housing service to Tipton, kept the Walsall

The Westland Homes scheme in Rowleys Green Lane, Coventry in the 1980s.

office for a while and there was this present office in Darlaston. West Bromwich was chosen as the centre because as it was in the middle of the two organisations it was fairer for staff and was right on the motorway junctions. You could get to your schemes quite easily.

I think property-wise we had about the same as Walsall Parklands but they had more staff and a bigger development team. Westland only had one person doing that and a clerk of works. I think the good thing was that the merger was very friendly and it was more like a family. It was a positive merger. Over the years we've moved on since then and other organisations have come into the Group. When you think that we've now got 11,000 properties and over 1,000 members of staff and when you look back over 30 years we started with ten people for about 500 properties. It's been a huge change.

We have to keep up to date with ever-changing legislation through Government, so that we can pass that knowledge on to our customers and also in house with our staff, as lots of them need to learn new skills. It's ever evolving. Should we actually be looking more at education and working in schools when children are younger to talk to them about housing and money? We are there for support and guidance.

Our accommodation is really diverse compared to what it was when we started. We probably had one-bedroomed flats, two-bedroomed flats and three-bedroom houses and that was it – and perhaps a few for the elderly like category ones where they'd got an alarm system to the local authority. Thirty years ago there were a lot of people we couldn't help, whereas now we help people from sixteen through to 100. Whatever the age group and whatever their need is we can actually find something for them to move to.

Queuing for Properties
Jane Irwin, Housing Officer

I left school when I was sixteen and was looking for a job. Westland was one of the interviews that I went for and I was offered a job as an office junior. It was 1979 and at that time the office was above a hairdresser's in Bearwood on Hagley Road. There were only seven or eight of us working there. That was it, that was all there was. It was terrifying to start with because I'd never had a job before. We weren't worldly-wise like the kids these days.

I remember the first week I was there I was given some filing to do. I went to find the files and there was no file in the pocket. So I thought 'I'll be clever here, I'll get some blank ones and I'll make a file' – because when we were at college we were taught that if you took a file out you put a card in that said who'd got the file. Well they didn't do that there, so there was a file somewhere that just happened to be on the floor on the side of somebody's desk. I thought I was being clever doing that but obviously I wasn't.

I don't think in those days we knew really what housing associations were, it was just a job that you did and you just had training in what you did as a role. When I was an office junior I was sent to college in the beginning to do shorthand. It was an evening course – but they wouldn't send you on anything that was housing related. You were just the junior and that's what you did.

I think when people saw properties built that then generated customers. We had 37 properties in one scheme in Halesowen, mostly houses and five flats. Because we were just down the road people would see the development with a board up saying Housing Corporation and then Westland and they'd come down to find out what was going on, to find out how they could get one of these houses.

When I first started we were only in Bearwood for a few months and then we moved to the offices at Link House in Rumbow, Halesowen. We started off with a really small office on the fourth floor of the building with another two companies. Over the years we took over extra bits and increased to several housing officers and we were squashed in.

Building 26 flats for elderly people for Westland Homes at Cwerne Court in Abbey Street, Gornal Wood in 1986.

I went on to become involved with retirement housing for sale. We got involved with Cox Homes, who built our first scheme in Westland Gardens, Stourbridge. It was 31 bungalows for sale to elderly people at 70% of the market value to enable elderly people to trade down to something smaller and have some money to live on. I remember when we came to sell those they were really popular and we had a lot of people interested in them. We were going to take reservations for them as a few of them wanted the same plot and they needed to come and pay a deposit.

On the day before we came to take deposits, we had people queuing outside because they wanted plot number so and so. I remember the chief executive, Gerry, saying he couldn't possibly have people sat outside all night; so we had to go out and get some raffle tickets and give them a raffle ticket with a number so that they could come at nine o'clock the next morning and reserve the one they wanted.

We had to have a service charge budget and I enjoyed doing that, and I still enjoy it today – the figures side of it. We employed a scheme manager and people to cut the grass, clean the windows and do other things. We did maintenance to the outside of the properties, and serviced the gas boilers. Anything else inside the property they were responsible for but we did the rest and collected the quarterly service charge for all of that.

It's the same now with servicing properties. I have to go to a residents' meeting every year and account for what we've spent the money on. The accounts are done properly and audited and then you have to present a budget for the coming year and explain why you think, perhaps, for the coming year their service charge needs to go up because this is the work that needs to be done over that year and in forthcoming years. You have to save so much money into a provision fund so that when the roofs need repairing then the money is there and you don't go back to them.

Since then I think I've worked in every department apart from regeneration. I've worked in IT, repairs and finance. As I moved through different jobs I got a better understanding of how the different departments worked and I think everyone knows these days what housing associations are.

Chapter 5

CO-OPERATION AND CONFIDENCE: BCHS

Carl Taylor, Director of Birmingham Co-operative Housing Services and Redditch Co-operative Homes

Empowering Communities

Today bchs is an agency that provides housing services to co-operatives. We only own 98 properties ourselves. The properties that we manage and support are owned by the co-operatives themselves. We work with nine Co-operatives for which we provide direct management services. They include Victoria, Triangle, 20/20, Balsall Heath, Shajalal, Bordesley Green, South Road, and Alpha in Birmingham and Paddock in Walsall. In addition we are actively involved in the exciting Redditch Homes Co-operative, and we have informal links with some other co-ops, Starling Housing Co-operative in Coventry for example.

We have a liaison officer that attends each one of the monthly meetings of the Co-operatives. The tenants sit and discuss their rent report or their repairs report or their development reports if they have developments – all the issues that are going on in their neighbourhood and their community.

They then create a set of actions which our liaison officers take back to bchs and which we implement over the next month. We will work round things like making sure that the rent for that co-operative is paid, and making sure that it has the repairs service that it wants. There will be other broader community things that we will be working on as well.

In bchs there is a staff of thirteen and in Redditch a staff of three. Some of the staff have a standard housing officer role; some of them have got a financial role for the community enterprises that co-operatives are; some of them have got the liaison role; and one or two of them, like me, have a management role.

It's critical that we get out and meet the tenants. I soon know if I am straying from the correct path because we have a very empowered group of residents who have been managing their own community enterprises for 30 to 40 years. Those community enterprises have developed into significant

Members of the Shajalal Housing Co-operative outside some of their new homes. It traced its origins to three earlier co-operatives for Bangladeshi people in Birmingham. The first was the Frederick Road Friendly Co-operative that was started in 1976 in Aston, mainly by people from Sylhet. It was a pioneering BME housing initiative and it opened its first scheme of 21 homes in the 1980s. That decade two other Bangladeshi housing co-operatives were formed: Aston Widows and Villa Park, which went on to own 54 properties between them by the end of the 1980s. Today Shajalal Housing Co-operative is one of the bchs co-operatives.

assets to their local community and they know how to tell you when things aren't right. There is a board that runs bchs itself. The co-operatives that we work with put a person on the Board and it makes the strategic decisions about how bchs goes forward.

As for me, I became involved with housing after I left university when I got a job for Sandwell Council involving regeneration on an estate. A Housing Action Trust was proposed for that area. It was meant to be a brave new world in which tenants would be involved in the processes, but I became disillusioned in terms of the lack control that tenants actually had in their housing. I wanted to see a different way of doing things and I saw that in Birmingham Co-operative Housing Services.

A bchs AGM and multi-cultural day at The Bond in Birmingham, thanks to Dennis Neale.

When they advertised a post in 1991 I applied for it and got it. By then, I had already started to develop my ideas of tenant-led housing. I was against regeneration projects that just rode through and did whatever they wanted to people. I felt that there was something wrong when you were involving people in how their houses were to be redeveloped and then they went along to meetings to discover that the architects had redesigned the estate and took their houses out without even talking to them. They would just sit the tenants in a big meeting and tell them, 'this is how it's going to be'.

I realised that there was something wrong there, but I didn't necessarily know the best way that tenants could be involved in influencing their housing until I actually started working for bchs. There I saw tenants coming together, forming their own companies, taking ownership collectively – and that was a much better way of running housing in this country.

The first meeting of a housing co-operative that I went to was at the Paddock Housing Co-operative in Walsall. I sat in the bottom of a block of flats and the tenants came in from work and they were talking about how they were going to knock down a disused garage and transform it for their community. They talked about how they were going to raise the finances for it and what they wanted to see put there. That was such a different world to the one where I'd been before. I realised that co-operatives were a much better way for society.

It was incredibly liberating and empowering for the community. There were people at that meeting who talked about how they had children and that they couldn't take them out because they lived at the top of blocks of flats. It must have been incredibly empowering to be able to get their co-operative to build houses with back gardens so that their children could play in them. They designed the houses and they were telling the architect what he should do and how they should be like. They were also negotiating with planning officers, and that's exactly how housing should be.

Tenants' Control

There were examples in the late 1970s and 1980s of tenants rebelling against a top-down process that was driven by professionals. In Birmingham, in Small Heath and in parts of Handsworth, this rebellion led to the creation of the Victoria Tenants' Co-op and the South Road Housing Co-op. Groups of ordinary working-class people were having their streets declared as unfit under the Urban Renewal process. They were living with private landlords, often in terrible conditions, and these tenants wanted to do something different in the area. So they came together, formed housing co-operatives, accessed social housing grants and took control of their houses collectively.

It wasn't easy for working-class people to do that because the Council had its own way of doing things, although for a short period Birmingham Council did become very supportive of those housing co-operatives. And the Government was also fairly supportive for a short period of time. But ordinary people had to be prepared to be very dedicated, to give up their nights, to work with architects, to put together plans, and to go to this meeting and that meeting with this officer or this person from the Housing Corporation. So it was never an easy task to form a housing co-operative.

In Small Heath, the Victoria Housing Co-operative started from a group of people living in Victoria Road, where a large number of properties were owned by a notorious private landlord and were in a very poor condition. What bchs did was to work with the tenants in order to form a co-operative. The co-operative then bought the private landlord out by gaining a social housing grant from the Housing Corporation.

This co-op was the best option for those tenants. They went from a situation where they had a private landlord who was telling them what to do to being their own landlord – and that's the critical thing about co-operative housing. So it was the best option for them but it was also the only option for them because council housing was being cut back and both housing association expenditure and the number of housing associations was significantly lower than it is now.

The Victoria Housing Co-operative modernised and renovated the properties. Then as people on the committee got older, it developed a scheme for older people; and as families grew in the co-operative, it did a development for family housing. The co-operative went on from that initial development for people who had been living in incredibly poor conditions and now we continue to support it as it provides its housing services to 134 households in the Small Heath area.

Birmingham Co-operative Housing Services itself was formed in 1984 from a couple of urban renewal projects, one in Small Heath and one in Handsworth. Shush and Hush I think they were called – Small Heath Co-operative Housing Services and Handsworth Co-operative Housing Services. These had developed from the urban renewal projects through giving advice to tenants and helping them to set up the housing co-operatives.

The co-operative movement itself had some supporters in Birmingham, and the leader of the Council, Sir Dick Knowles, was a co-operator and was very involved in the co-operative movement. He wanted to see co-operative housing developed in the City. As an advocate of co-operative housing he used Urban Renewal as a way of enabling that message to get across.

But bchs also came from the co-operative movement itself. A man called Howard Campbell went to Scandinavia, saw co-operative housing and wanted to bring the idea back to Britain. He produced the Campbell Report for the 1974-79 Labour Government and that provided the impetus for co-operative housing in this country.

The initiatives wouldn't have succeeded, though, if co-operative housing hadn't been embraced by and addressed the needs of ordinary people like those in Victoria Road, Small Heath. However, the 1989 Housing Act changed the environment again for housing co-operatives and it became much harder for them to develop. The Act meant that rather than having a grant available to develop a house, housing associations now had to compete for that grant; and the way that housing associations competed for that grant was by increasing the rents of all the tenants.

If you had to sit in front of a room full of tenants and say, 'we want to develop some more housing because there is a housing need in this area' then they would say, 'yes we agree completely'. Then if we said, 'and you will all have to pay an extra £5 for the privilege', that would be a different story.

You can understand why, because we were talking and working with the poorest communities and they were saying, and I think they were right, 'it isn't the poorest communities that should be paying to house the poorest communities. It should be the whole of society that pays to house the poorest communities'.

So the 1989 Housing Act and its introduction of competition for the grant rate really made it very, very difficult for the housing co-operatives in Birmingham to continue to develop – although in Walsall we managed to do so. There was less competition there and also we were developing our partnership with Accord, which allowed us to carry out some development.

A bchs away weekend at Trafford Hall with the late Terry Edis in the blue polo shirt in the middle; thanks to Dennis Neale. Terry Edis was the Chair of Burrowes Street Resident Association, and then Burrowes Street Co-operative. He went on to also chair bchs and WATMOS, and was a fierce advocate of tenant control as well as an extremely skilful negotiator.

In Birmingham, however, the competition was much fiercer around social housing and grant rates.

After that phase of urban renewal in Birmingham, I went on to work for Redditch Co-operative Homes. This was purposely set up to establish housing co-operatives in the town that were democratically accountable to the people. We involved the residents in design and we had some meetings where there would be 50 people in a room. The builders would then come along and talk about the central heating system that was going in and the tenants would think that was fantastic.

Then the secondary fire place was mentioned and this was the standard three-bar electric fire. And we would say, 'is this okay for you?' and tenants didn't have the confidence necessarily to challenge that three-bar fire. They would say, 'yes that's fine' and then we would have to get that changed once the builders had gone and we had the real conversation. We would say to the tenants, 'did you really like that?' and they would say, 'no, but we didn't know we could say no'.

Three-bar fires were institutional, almost a badge of social housing at the time – and that's not what people wanted. People wanted to be proud of their house. And by being involved in the design of their house they could shape their house in a way they could be proud of. The three-bar electric fire was anathema to that whole concept. So it was about building tenants' confidence for them to be able to say what they wanted and what they thought was appropriate for their housing.

If you look at Redditch Co-operative Homes or bchs now you will find that the vast majority of staff are from the co-operative housing group that they have adopted themselves. They had those skills there latently but they needed to be developed and supported and the training that is provided by co-operatives enables people to do that.

In Redditch Co-operative Homes all the staff started off as young tenants in flats and they have gone on to blossom and become very capable officers. We've also got people who've gone on to become school teachers and independent financial advisers because of the confidence they've gained from doing co-operative housing training.

You cannot have a co-operative society without working with the whole neighbourhood because the people that know best about their housing are the people who live in their housing. The thing about co-operative housing is that the people who live in their housing control the companies. They take a holistic approach and you can't enable a co-operative to operate without providing the education, training and support to that co-operative.

So co-operatives were very much ahead of the game and still are in terms of empowering communities to be able to make the decisions that they want. Co-operatives are the only sorts of housing where the tenants themselves actually control the budgets that are being decided. Housing co-operatives change the power relationship and turn it on its head. Rather than the likes of me, housing professionals, thinking they know best at making the decisions it now becomes the people that live in those houses that are making the decisions about their housing. That's the critical thing about co-operative housing.

Often the tenants will disagree with me. In the last couple of years we had a big discussion with one of our co-operatives about whether or not timber windows should be put in. I was arguing that they should be as they're more environmentally friendly, but the co-operative said no. They wanted upvc windows because they need less maintenance and they were more effective for their budget. That meant that they could spend their money on doing other things to improve the area in a much better way.

That's how it should work. It shouldn't be about me saying that I think the environment is one of the most important issues in choosing windows; it should be the tenants deciding what the most important thing is for them. That is the only way that we shall really change the communities we live in for the better.

Tenant Management with Accord

Very early in the 1990s Birmingham Co-operative Housing Services merged with the Accord Group. It merged because it was looking for an answer on how to address the question 'how do we develop in this new climate where there is competition for grants?' The solution was to join a bigger housing association with resources that could support bchs in developing new ideas.

Ethos was critical to the merger. It was important that we joined an organisation that respected co-operative values and principles. And there was a choice for bchs. We had a 'beauty parade' before we joined the Accord Group. The senior management at the time didn't want to join. Their aim was to join a bigger organisation with more stock in Birmingham – and Accord at that time had more stock in Walsall.

But our co-operators saw that fact as a strategic advantage and they also felt that the Accord management, Chris Handy in particular, would have more of a passion for co-operative housing. They wanted to join an organisation that would allow co-operative ideas to develop and flourish and would support and nourish them. So the people that lived in our properties, the people that made the decision because we are co-operative housing, the tenants – they did want to join Accord.

I think the co-operators have been proved right. Accord have been true to their word all the way through. They haven't interfered within the management of bchs; they've supported bchs; they've allowed bchs to go and develop where that was possible; and they've created Redditch Co-operative Homes as a new co-operative vehicle. If you look at other mergers that took place at a similar time with other housing organisations, then those smaller organisations no longer exist and have been long forgotten.

In the 90s there was some small-scale development of those existing housing co-operatives which was carried out by buying properties in and around the communities where they operated. For example, Bordesley Green developed Prince Regent Close; Victoria bought some Existing Satisfactory

The committee of the Ragley Tenant Management Co-operative opening their scheme at Ragley Close, Bloxwich on 11 November 1994. The scheme consisted of 22 two and three-bedroomed houses and was managed by the tenants on a co-operative basis. This was the first freestanding Tenant Managed Co-operative in a housing association in the West Midlands and the tenants were helped by bchs to learn to manage their homes.

Dwellings as they were called. These were houses that didn't need a lot of work on them as they had been improved somewhere along the way.

Additionally, bchs worked as a consultant to support tenants in council housing to take control of their housing. In particular, we spent a lot of time developing the organisations that went on to become WATMOS Housing Co-operative in Walsall, which took ownership of just under 2,000 council properties when the stock transfer of council houses happened. So we worked with a lot of the Walsall tenants' management co-operatives like those in Burrowes Street, The Avenues and Chuckery.

I remember going to Burrowes Street and talking to a group of residents there. They were saying that the only way that they could get a repair done was if they took the council to court. That was the only repair book that the council had at the time and that was crazy. Nobody wanted to take the council to court to get their repairs done; they just wanted a decent repairs service.

So we sat down and worked with a group of tenants to create a tenants' management co-operative on Burrowes Street. It had the same amount of money that the council had been spending on that estate previously but it was able to transform it by not having to spend several thousand pounds on a solicitor in order to change the locks on a property. That made a big difference to that estate and to other estates in Walsall. We were also very involved in that movement for tenant control in Walsall, and we've also done some of that in Sandwell, in Wolverhampton, in Dudley and Birmingham.

As a result of the merger with Accord, bchs was also able to develop an expertise around Self-Build Housing. This was clearly a neat fit for the Co-operative housing ethos with our values of self-help and self-responsibility. Our first self-build scheme was in Walsall with the Walsall Homemakers. We recruited a group of unemployed people and gave them some tools and a site manager and said, 'right off you go'. It wasn't always plain sailing and we experimented with timber frame products in order to make the construction process simpler. But both we and the self-builders learnt a lot from the process.

We carried on this expertise to carry out more self-build schemes through the west midlands to the point where we became the experts in self-build housing across the region. We developed some really high quality self-build schemes, with projects such as those in Walsall, Castle Vale, Redditch and famously the one televised at Bordesley by Kevin McCloud.

We have also adapted and refined ideas around self-build housing so that we developed concepts such as train and build, whereby the focus was more on getting people work ready rather than achieving a 'sweat-equity'.

Working on the Bordesley Leisure Gardens self-build scheme with Kevin McCloud of the Channel 4 television programme 'Grand Designs'.

As the economy picked up and employment improved, self-build housing became less of a priority for people. But now that we are back in recession and with rising unemployment, ideas around self-build housing are returning to the fore again. Today we can offer a range of self-build products from very traditional self-builds, where skilled people come together and share the house building process and make a sweat-equity, to developments with a focus on training and employability through train and build. There are also schemes that utilise our new timber frame factory to facilitate the development side of self-commissioned housing.

Innovative Ideas: Redditch Co-operative Homes

It is incredibly difficult to fund the work of housing co-operatives. The introduction of competition for grant rate made things very difficult, but bchs has looked at ways of overcoming that through developing leasehold models of co-operatives. So we've created Redditch Co-operative Homes, which was set up in partnership with Accord and the local authority.

In 1997 Redditch Borough Council thought it would be able to develop council housing when the new Labour Government was elected, but it wasn't able to do so. The local authority then thought about how it could provide affordable housing. It held a competition in the late 90s to see who could provide the most practically accountable form of housing.

We in bchs were successful in winning that competition. As a result of that we have developed over 300 properties in Redditch in five new neighbourhood co-operatives. We have also used the resources of Accord, because the homes are transferred into Redditch Co-operative Homes in order to provide leases to co-operatives that then manage the properties on a day-to-day basis.

If you move into one of the leasehold properties, and as with other housing co-operatives, you can go to the meetings. The meetings make all

Riverside Housing Co-operative handing over this playground to Redditch Borough Council on 3 August 2011. On the left is Councillor Bill Hartnett chairman of Redditch Borough Council. To the right is the late Ken Somner, a long-serving Labour councillor and former mayor of Redditch and also chair of Redditch Co-operative Homes. Ken was a passionate believer in co-operative housing and became the founding chair of Redditch Co-operative Homes and a founder member of Breedon Housing Co-operative.

the decisions and the tenants still control the budget. The difference is in where the freehold of the property lies. In the Victoria Housing Co-operative in Small Heath the freehold of the property lies with Victoria itself because it was able to afford to buy the freehold; whereas in Redditch what we've done is to pool the freeholds of those co-operatives in Redditch Co-operative Homes to allow us to develop in the new environment.

We've got Pioneer Housing Co-operative, Riverside Housing Co-operative, Winyates Co-operative, Breedon Housing Co-operative and Redditch Co-operative 2000. We've got these co-operatives to co-operate with each other with the freeholds to facilitate other developments. We have had to innovate to create solutions to legislation and changes in regulation designed to drive for better efficiencies in the provision of social housing. They have not been designed to stop co-operative housing but that has been a by-product.

So the 1990s was a time of growth round tenant management, whilst the 2000s was when we grew Redditch Co-operative Homes. This was a really exciting new co-operative vehicle and was really empowering for the people who got involved with it. We are hoping for the 'teens', the 2010s, to see the development of mutual home ownership. This is the most common form of co-operative housing in the world, and co-operative housing is very common in the rest of the world.

The model they use is a shared equity co-operative. We think that there is a lot of mileage in that, particularly in the current climate where it is very hard for people to enter the housing market on their own. You need a 20% deposit for a property and you need to have absolutely no debt – and that's very difficult for families to achieve. By contrast, a shared equity co-op would require a small share purchase as a deposit to move into the property and a rental payment. It is very attractive model of going forward for new housing developments.

This model allows someone to buy more shares as time goes on but in the collective of properties.

Lord Ted Graham of Edmonton, Honorary President of Redditch Co-operative Homes presenting a training certificate to Co-operative member Adrian Elgie.

Instead of buying shares in an individual house they are buying shares in their neighbourhood, and so they're investing in their community. They can also sell those shares. Generally speaking a valuation is taken and the organisation has the first right to buy back the shares; if they don't buy them back the person has the right to sell the shares on the open market.

Throughout that period of the early 90s there was this climate of demutualisation on a massive scale across the rest of the co-operative movement. There were attempts to demutualise supermarkets which were defeated, but we saw building society after building society demutualised. Those demutualised societies went on to be the organisations that helped create the financial crisis we find ourselves in through acting in a cavalier fashion.

History has shown that mutualism works because the organisations that didn't demutualise have probably been our salvation in this financial crisis. I think that has caused a change in people's attitudes to the value of what can be achieved by working together. That is what mutualism and co-operation is about.

A Paddock Co-operator
Margaret Cope, board member bchs and Accord Group

I am a member of Paddock Co-op and also on the boards of bchs and Accord. With bchs and members of our co-op we introduced Tenant Managed Organisations (TMOs) to Walsall and then Accord and bchs asked if we would meet the people in Redditch, which I believe was the start of Redditch Co-operative Homes when this co-op started. I was asked to join the board and for two to three years used to go to visit and encourage the members in Redditch and I feel it was a successful project.

I was asked to come back to the bchs Board and I believe it to be a good place and I have been to activities at Accord. I also met the Moseley and District Churches Housing Association people before they joined the family and also the Caldmore people. I still like to think I have a place in the activities of all the different projects that are happening and best of all making people aware of co-ops and the people who live and help to run them.

Proud to be Co-operative
Chrissie Muirhead, Resident Involvement Officer
Tenant and Co-operator

In 1980 my husband, Tony, and I and our oldest daughter were living in short-life accommodation in Nechells that was due to be pulled down. Housing associations and other landlords housed people in properties like this knowing there was a six to twelve-month life span before there was a compulsory purchase order. We were with Friendship as it was known then, and we had been in a council flat in Castle Bromwich before we moved into the house in Nechells.

The conditions were terrible. The windows didn't close upstairs because the walls had subsided. There were cracks in the walls. The floorboards never met the skirting boards, so you couldn't put mats down or carpets. Sanitary wise it was alright. Everything worked but it was on the end of a block that had already been knocked down and the houses across the road were already boarded up ready for demolition.

Even though we didn't criticise it too much, it was short term and we knew that we were going to be moved on. It was just that we couldn't make it home. We couldn't furnish it and you didn't decorate because you knew it would be a waste of time. We were offered somewhere over in Balsall Heath but we wanted to come to Small Heath as that's where my husband is from.

My husband was working for The Shape Trust and they were working with the Balsall Heath Housing Co-operative. Someone he was working with said why don't you get an application form and get involved with housing co-ops. We knew there were a couple of co-ops in Small Heath that had been started, particularly Victoria, and that's where we wanted to get back to. But there were no application forms so I kept on ringing up every week, and I just kept saying, 'Don't forget we're interested in getting involved with the co-op'.

In those days you became a member of the co-op before you became a tenant, because there were only a certain amount of properties and they wanted people who were going to be in the co-operative spirit and get involved. Victoria had only just got started in 1978 or 79. When Tony and I joined there were only about 15 houses in the co-op.

Anyway, I pushed every single week, I was on the phone. When we actually got our appointment I was to speak with someone called Chris Ellis. He was from Bradford and when we went for our interview at Osborne House on the Coventry Road, as he opened the door to me he said, 'I don't have to ask your name, I can tell who you are, you've been on the phone to me every week!'

Anyway we had an interview and we were successful. We then worked voluntarily for six or seven months on the management committee, going to meetings and playing various roles such as secretarial or financial. Then we were offered a property in September 1981, and we now had two children. We'd been living in poor conditions by today's standards but the house that the Co-op gave us was an absolute palace. It had central heating, an inside toilet and a bathroom.

It was a refurb, so it was an old three-bedroomed terraced house in Victoria Avenue off Glovers Road. The co-op were given a Housing Association Grant from the Housing Corporation and the house was completely done out. We had a brand-new bathroom and toilet on the back where they'd built the extension. The kitchen was all brand new, brand-new central heating, and new windows. Urban Renewal was coming along at the time and doing the roofs. It was like a palace and everybody in both our families were really pleased for us because we were the first ones with central heating. It was just a lovely, lovely home.

We thought we'd won the pools because it was posh. It was beautiful to say the least and you'd got a choice. So for the front-room gas fire there was a choice of three from the contractors, because it was staff from Midland Area who were doing the refurbing. They actually came to our house over in Nechells and brought us the pattern books for wallpaper. You felt like you were included.

I carried on voluntary work on the management committee for up to sixteen years afterwards. Before then the only thing I knew about co-ops was our divi number and the co-op up the Soho Road. That was all, but I learnt about what co-ops were. I learnt that it was about people coming together and helping out and just being their own landlords. We interviewed prospective tenants and one of our women tenants collected the rent.

The Avenue was predominantly Bangladeshi and Pakistani families. It was a nice community feel as all the kids played together. It was very important to get South Asian folk involved in the Co-op as we knew that there was a need for larger properties for them. When the Byron Road development came along we were able to build four and five bedroomed homes. I was part of the committee on the development side and we built properties that had a ground-floor bedroom for elderly parents so that they could come and move in with their families.

They were beautiful homes. That's why we built those size properties for people, for Asian families and anybody else to have somewhere decent to live. There were a lot of people on the waiting list that needed that size of properties. It was just lovely to be able to say, 'we're building these houses and you can move in and your family can move in'. Two or three generations could move in and live there.

The co-operative ideal became extremely important to me. It was everything. It was something that I was proud to be in; it was something that

I knew provided good housing; and it provided a base. We had an office at 26 Grange Road, the first office, and it was somewhere you could just go in after taking the kids to school, see someone and have a natter. Somebody might need a hand with something and it was like a community centre.

I carried on going to the meetings, became secretary and attended general meetings. Victoria just grew and grew, and we'd go to auctions and buy houses in auctions. We also had a lot of development at the time. In 1982/83 we were building flats and houses in Lloyd Street, Wordsworth Road, and Victoria House. It was exciting. We were bringing people into the Co-op, interviewing people and going to the places where they lived – and most times they were just like where Tony and I had lived. I liked that part of it. I like including people, knowing they're going to get something good.

So it was going to site meetings and going to meetings with the development team, the builders and others. Every day there was something to do. The people that we met from Midland Heart, like Bob Daniels, and

Nick Raynsford, then Housing Minister, visiting the Train and Build scheme at Parsons Road, Redditch; he is accompanied by Carl Taylor of bchs and Redditch Co-operative Homes. The development is now part of Pioneer Co-operative and allowed young vulnerable people to achieve a qualification whilst building their homes. Several of the young people continued into apprenticeships and two returned to work on future sites such as Yarr Mill Close.

Ruth Miller from Focus and people like that were just lovely people. Even though they were professionals there was no sort of hierarchy with them having an education and us not having gone to a university. It was really relaxed and everybody got on. They were just friends and you could go to the pub with them and go on social events.

As secretary I was sending out notices, taking the minutes, typing them up at home – the Co-op provided an electric typewriter – and I'd go up to the office then and photocopy them. I'd arrange general meetings and AGMs. And you learned people skills, like being able to talk to a group of people round a table – something which you'd never thought of before. I know what it's like to feel nervous so if I meet someone for the first time I tried to make them feel comfortable.

Then in the early 90s Victoria got some ESD money. There was no building going on but you could get Existing Satisfactory Dwelling grant. That meant you could buy properties from the open market. We had a bit of friendly rivalry with other co-ops nearby, so you had Triangle up by Wright Street in Small Heath and then Blake Lane Co-op got some money for some of these ESD houses.

So myself and Angela Healey, God rest her soul, we left our kids with our husbands and we'd get on the bus and we'd go to these road shows that the Housing Corporation were putting on round the West Midlands because we wanted some of these ESD houses. I think Philip Champness, he was head of the Housing Corporation in those days, must have thought he had two mad stalkers because there was myself and Angela front row at as many of the road shows we could get to. Anyway we got the money for Victoria's first nine ESDs. It was a passion.

A Changed Life

In 1997 I was doing an 'A' level as a mature student at Sheldon Heath School and I was working as a cleaner at Severn Trent. I was asked if I would be interested in a job which included managing the diary of the PA to the C o E, as she was abroad a lot with the company's charity Water Aid. Sheldon Heath's head teacher approached me and said he was applying for some funding to employ people as classroom mentors and would I be interested in an interview. Then this job came up at bchs and I applied for it.

I had to do a fifteen-minute presentation, which I'd never done before, there were four people on the interviewing panel. I'd known these people through the Co-op. Two them were managers and two of them were volunteers. My presentation was about committee skills, how to run a committee meeting. I thought I could do the job but I didn't think I would get it. But I did and I started in November 1997 as a liaison officer for the committee. Anybody that knew me before I joined the co-op knew I wasn't a talkative person. I was very quiet, very shy. But it brought me out of myself, as it did for a lot of girls I know now. I've come up through the co-ops. I've worked at bchs now for fifteen years, the co-op offered me an opportunity to find work as well. I've been to college with the Co-op, I've been on training courses and so it's developed my personal skills – and those of my children as well, because they've took part. They've gone away on day trips and gone away for the weekend.

There was a scheme called TIS, Tenants' Incentive Scheme, which the Government introduced. If you found a property on the open market your landlord would give you £9,000 towards buying it and then your old property would go to someone on the council's waiting list. Many people I know took TIS but it was never for me and Tony, it was never an option. We've had three houses over 30 years and our house now in Yardley is where we've been for nineteen years and it's wonderful, absolutely wonderful.

Without exaggerating in any shape or form, the Co-op has changed our life. I don't know where we would have been. I can't even think about it, because it's for me and if we have an opportunity to develop in the future – and I know things are difficult at the moment – I would love to move into something smaller for us to retire into. We've got flats in Henshaw Road, Small Heath for mature people and if necessary we'll give up our house and move into a smaller place. So there's the option there to stay within the Co-op.

I'm a resident involvement officer and I work for four housing co-ops. That means I get involved with tenants and I do tenancy support. The policy is that we interview three people for each property and we have about six questions that we ask everybody so that it's fair – about living in communities, how you feel about neighbours, what's your interpretation of anti-social behaviour, how you feel about co-ops. Then we do settling in visits, over the first few months, to people who have moved in. I've worked with every co-op that has its services from bchs and I think the fact that I am a tenant as well is the basis of how I see the job and do the job.

There are a lot of people who have been given a lot of opportunities through bchs. I am passionate about it and I am extremely proud of it. I think we are an excellent organisation and it is a family. We understand people. It's there for co-operatives, and over the years we've had co-ops from around the country come to us for advice on various policies and procedures.

A Reluctant Volunteer

Dennis Neale Treasurer, Alpha Housing Co-operative Ltd.

It's a rather large task, picking from over thirty-four years of accumulated memories. The start, of course, is easy to deal with. Losing Inner City Partnership money forced the various co-operative groups to rethink, and reevaluate their positions. For each group to fund their own service levels, most being fledgling organisations, was not an option, so the secondary co-ops, under which umbrella they operated, amalgamated into one – Birmingham Co-operative Housing Services Ltd.

This not only brought together primary co-operatives from across the City, but enabled some limited funding to spread the idea and start others. Managing and maintaining the idea of self-determination, though, is not an easy thing to do, and for some time we were all looked on as a bunch of non-conformers. Fair enough, I always thought, we were. Believing that a well-trained group could achieve, if not better, the housing conditions offered by local authorities, we have, by and large, proved to be correct.

The movement, though, has long been eclipsed by the growth of many housing associations, and arms-length housing companies. We still have a great many things to offer our local communities, though, as we have always done – such as a friendly and efficient service, prompt repairs, and an interest in our members' lives and families.

As to picking out a specific memory, I am still struggling, there have been so many. The famous, (and to some, infamous) bchs weekend away, was always a high point in the year. With at times, over twenty workshops to choose from, it could be a very tiring experience, even spread over three days.

The visit to Denmark, mixed with a selection of the UK's best housing association staff, brings back many memories. A notable one is being told not to turn left, when venturing out of the hotel, otherwise we would be in the so called 'adult' section of Copenhagen. No I never did (well ok, maybe a little peek).

Dublin was a sheer delight, the friendly atmosphere, the warmth of welcome, and I haven't even mentioned the beer. While being shown round a notorious Dublin estate, I happened to remark on the concrete ramps at the base of some tower blocks. Assuming they were to aid the disabled, I was mortified to hear that they had been constructed illegally, so that trotting horses could be stabled on the second or third floors. I may, from time to time, complain about my own co-operatives tenants, thankfully, not about horses.

There are many other places and memories that spring to mind, but the abiding overall memory is of the people. Whether it was staff, tenants, or other like-minded volunteers, the help and politeness has always stood out. A great many years on various committees, at THACH, bchs, Accord, and my own, Alpha Housing Co-operative, has resulted in some long term friendships, which continue to this day.

I did think, many years past, that I would have long ago retired from what I call the 'sharp end' of social housing. But no, here I am again, belting out yet more recollections of my past, although thankfully, I have not included any names or embarrassing events. It's all been a fairly happy adventure, and I remain grateful for the opportunities bchs has provided over the years. It would be wrong to say in summing up, that it's been an easy ride, it hasn't, most organisations have their ups and downs, but it's survived, and that's the main thing.

Chapter 6

AN IDEAL MODEL: ASHRAM

Akshay Parikh: Chairman Accord Group

Starting the Journey

Originally my grandfather was from Gujarat in India but in the late 1890s/early 1900s they went into East Africa working on the railways there. My great uncle then went into the teaching profession and my father followed him, becoming a lecturer in Kenya. Then in 1975, because of the issues of Uganda and Africanisation, we emigrated to the UK because we had the right of access.

I graduated from the University of London and started a career in banking in the 1980s. I came to Birmingham and worked for Midland Bank here and my first contact with housing associations was with Ashram. I was approached by the Birmingham Chamber of Commerce as well as two or three key individuals who were at that time associated with the Moseley and District Housing Association. They came to me and said 'we have heard about you, you work for a bank, we understand from the Chamber that you have some views and some leadership qualities. We have recently commissioned a study into the Asian community and how the Asian elderly in particular look after themselves and how there is a big disparity between the youth and the elderly around family cohesion.'

Increasingly the research was pointing towards tensions within the household because of family members working and their inability to look after their parents to the level that their expectations were. The parents' expectations were that as they grew older the children would by definition look after them. That was the family tradition. But this research found that whilst this still continued to be the ambition and the aspiration, the working patterns and the economic stresses in Birmingham in particular was causing a lot of tensions.

There was a view that would it be a good idea to set up a housing association which specifically catered for the cultural needs of the South Asian community. If we did that, would we be supported or would the perceptions about the Asian community and the elderly mitigate against us moving forward because it was seen as a taboo. How could we create an environment in which we were fostering a concept that as parents get elderly you can farm them away into another establishment?

That concept of a sheltered scheme provided by another was not there, it was not well embedded in the Asian culture. It was alien to the Asian culture and was seen as something of an abdication of the children's responsibility to look after their elderly parents. The culture very much is that when you are young your parents look after you and when the tables turn and they become older then you continue to look after them – as long as you have the means and the capabilities to do so. And by and large it was within the extended family environment that these relationships and tensions used to be managed.

There were three things actually at work. The economic forces – both husband and wife had to go out so who would look after the parents. Then there was the structure of the UK house itself the two-up two-down, wasn't that conducive to looking after elderly. As they got old stairs would become a big issue and if the couple had children where was the accommodation for the parents. In the traditional Asian home everything was scattered around the ground floor and it was rooms within rooms, as it were, but you couldn't do that here because of overcrowding issues and so on.

So the concept was this – would we be able to set up a specialist scheme primarily targeted at the South Asian population, and by that I mean the Indian, Pakistani and Bangladeshi community. People might say that might be seen as restrictive but we thought, 'let's try because we have a defined concept and let's see how far we can go with that to make it a reality'.

I would say to the guys, 'look you need some big money for this. You not only want to set up a sheltered scheme but you also need to raise money to run it. If we put a proposition that the cost of this scheme has to be fully borne by the family members then you're starting for failure because affordability would become an issue. So you need to start off with some Government support to make it happen.'

So we looked around and a housing association was an ideal model for us to begin to start on the journey. We started this discussion around 1990, 1991, 1992 and we approached the Housing Corporation as it was then to say, 'look we have this concept that is embedded in the research that has been commissioned by a university and was carried out by some eminent people in the sector and how would you respond if we were to approach the Housing Corporation to get registration status for a housing association catering for the needs?'

A site visit to Ghulab Ashram to see work underway to build extra care bungalows.

At that stage it fitted in with the Housing Corporation's BME (Black Minority Ethnic) agenda to promote and foster culturally sensitive housing options for people from the former Commonwealth countries that had settled in the UK. But there was a difficulty in that whilst the strategy was there the Government was almost on the verge of saying no more housing associations because there were enough of those.

At that stage I think there were about close to 2,000 registered housing associations. And Government was moving down the agenda and saying, 'actually not all of them are sustainable, what's the point of having disparate housing associations. Let's try and introduce efficiency measures and quality measures within the housing association movement. And instead of registering new ones let's get existing ones consolidated and drive for scale and quality.'

Well, we were certainly strong-minded in those days and we said 'no, no, no. If you said we were a division of another housing association the community wouldn't buy that.' They would want to see something that was driven by, administered by and led by people who understood their culture and affinity to their language.

So we lobbied hard and it was classic diplomacy really. The Housing Corporation said 'we want to support you in enabling this to happen but we can't because central government is saying we can't'. It was a sign of maturity in the team that we thought long and hard about how we could break the impasse. There was no point in us going to the press and saying 'we are a worthy cause and the government is refusing our registration', so what we did was play a clever game, a subtle game if I can put it that way.

We promoted a number of events where we invited key-note speakers and attendees and guests, including the local MPs and the Institute of Asian Business. And we created some noise, not just shouting, stating that 'this was a genuine cause and business and leaders within the Asian community are looking ten to fifteen years ahead. This is going to become a big issue for family cohesion, and rather than expose it let's manage this thing in a more mature way and educate people to say it's not a bad thing if you have to send your parents to an external organisation, as long as it is culturally sensitive in providing for the needs and you have an influence in the shape and the design and it's run by people you can trust.'

We created quite a lot of events in late 1993, 1994. We got the Chamber involved, we got the MPs involved, we got the local authority involved and we held events at Edgbaston Cricket ground which were sponsored by other housing associations. The Housing Association started to realise that what we were saying made sense and they should just let this one happen and then close the door!

A Place of Rest

We got through the door and we were registered in 1994 and I was part of the board of management. So we started the journey and the journey was quite difficult. There was great ambition, great support from local partners. We had a great storyboard to say we would do this, that and the other – but for ambition to be turned into reality requires a very strong team, requires funding, requires skilled people to deliver the scheme. And we had a lot of that.

It was an ambition that was driven because we had a belief in a proposition and an affinity to help the elderly who weren't getting a good deal in those days. And simple things like a Hindu and a Muslim staying within a care home: one is a vegetarian and one is a meat eater. They've got different praying times. In those days some of the well-established housing associations and care schemes weren't sensitive to the needs of different religions. Part of our job was to actually help people to understand the differences between the Asian communities and the segmentation.

In the end, and with partners, we developed about 150 housing units and we developed two care schemes: Ghulab Ashram in Hall Green and Kalyan Ashram in Sparkbrook. But we couldn't own any of that; we had to do it almost like a surrogate relationship with existing housing associations. That was because even though the Housing Corporation gave us the registration they weren't 100% confident that we would be capable of receiving grant directly and developing the schemes ourselves directly – because we had no experience.

So we had to have partners and the Housing Corporation actually was very good to us. They said, 'look we understand what you are doing but rather than give you the two million we will do it through a partner, who will be your local delivery partner. You influence the way they deliver that scheme for you, and we won't bother you with a lot of bureaucracy because of a lot of our money comes through bureaucracy and we would like you to grow.'

In a way it was a very strong enabling model. Some people thought that they didn't trust us but some of us said 'let's learn from this, we're not developers, we're not landowners'. And our ambition was not to be a landowner or a house owner. Our ambition was to make sure that the service delivery was sensitive to the needs of the residents and we had influence on the design of the building to design it appropriately.

The first project was about ten houses in Sparkhill and a care home, Ghulab Ashram. These were quite difficult for us simply because we realised that creating the infrastructure was difficult with the ground to lay out, the partners to build the scheme. Then we had to recruit, we had to make sure the staff were trained to meet the needs, that the staff themselves knew the differentiation between the various communities within the scheme.

We had quality embedded within the delivery process and to some extent we had to learn the ropes as the management team. We had to make sure we picked the right chief executive, we had the right care and support team and that the housing management services we were giving were sensitive to the needs of the community.

So the buildings were put up by our partner in consultation with ourselves; the design of the scheme was in consultation with ourselves; and the procurement of the contractor, the sub-contractor was in consultation with us. Because it was in consultation with us some of the schemes were designed to fit the Asian family and communities' environment.

Kalyan Ashram was very much a conversion of a church accommodation and we had to fit in with the heritage of the building; but Ghulab Ashram is

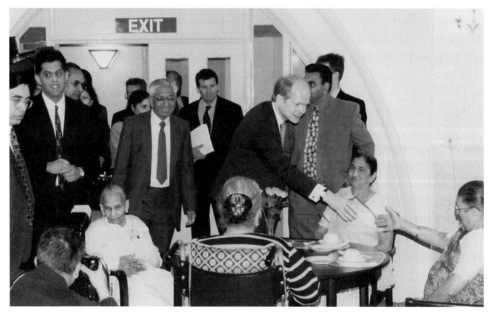

William Hague, former leader of the Conservative Party shaking hands with service users at Kalyan Ashram, which was Birmingham's first ever Asian elder extra care scheme (1996). Left of him is Naginbhi Parmar, former Chair of Ashram Board.

a designed provision which acknowledged that privacy was quite important. Asian families had lots of visitors coming in and there was always sensitivity around cooking and prayers.

So we designed the scheme so that there were individual self-contained units, each of which was effectively a bedsit or a one-bedroomed flat with their own access into the living area. It had common area that was ambient and well designed. That's where we conducted our initial classes, delivery of therapy. We wanted to ensure that the residents didn't just sit in front of the television and as internet technology came into the world we had classes on that as well.

We also had a nice garden area for the residents to relax and enjoy; and a communal eating area that again could meet the cultural differences of individuals. The difference was that initially there were different tables for different communities to sit round and eat. So the vegetarians would have their own table and did not have sit with meat eaters. There was also an opportunity for residents to cook their own food in their own units. They had a small cooking area if they wanted to use that or if they wanted to buy in from the main kitchen they could do that. So there was flexibility. There is a cost attached to that. If we were to say 'is the kitchen breaking even' then it's not – but it's for the scheme manager to identify other streams of funding to help support it or ask for donations.

We ensured that prayer rooms and prayer times were respected. We ensured that if there was a call out into a care room then if it was a lady a lady went in to bathe or attend to the needs. As far as we could, if it was a Hindu lady we would ensure that the care worker was the same.

There were plenty of care workers from the community but we had to make sure we weren't playing to the lobbies. We had to make sure they were properly trained and the training was on site. We worked alongside our partners and said 'do you have a care quality manager that we can borrow from you until we train ours up'. And we made sure that the staff recruitment had an affinity for the Asian community.

Very quickly we found that because we were taking time in talking to people to understand their needs and vice versa, we were suddenly becoming a much more attractive proposition to work in because we were seen as a different type of organisation. Interestingly, within three to four years of our establishment when we looked at the demographics and the ethnicity, we were attracting 25% of white residents and also some African Caribbean residents. They liked the environment, we were more sensitive to people's needs, we'd spend time and we listened.

A lot of that was enabled to happen because we had higher grant rates from the Housing Corporation. There was no magic about it, but we could afford a slightly better staff to resident ratio because we had proved the case that we needed slightly more because of the cultural sensitivities. By doing that we were becoming a preferred supplier of care.

Within a period of five years, if you looked at our staff mix, we were no longer a South Asian or BME organisation. You walked into Ghulab Ashram or some of our residential schemes and you'd think 'yeh the board says it's Ashram Housing Association, but the residents don't give you that impression because you'll get 60% Asian, 20-25% white, 15-20% African Caribbean. You looked around and looked at the staff and it was mixed.'

Some of the local councillors in Sparkhill and Sparkbrook couldn't understand that. The name was Hindi, non-Muslim and affiliated to the culture of India, as an ashram is a place of rest; and by and large the early senior staff were Hindus – but there was no taboo. We then started to realise the benefit of our specialism and we said, 'well actually there's no point in segregating ourselves as a BME, as an Asian organisation as here's an opportunity for all'. Whilst the original people who were behind the organisation were largely from India, they were Hindus and Sikhs, by years six and seven a significant proportion of our residents were Muslims.

Our houses were and are scattered around Sparkhill, Sparkbrook, and Kings Heath in Birmingham with some in Sandwell and Walsall. If you look around and say, 'why is this Ashram property?' then it's because there was land there and our development partner wanted us to be there. Most of our schemes are four to five bedroomed and designed to reflect that need for more space – because Asian families have five, six or seven members not three of four. And our gardens are not very big as Asians don't make good gardeners. Traditionally gardening wasn't something that they would do.

The kitchens are traditional, nothing specific around that – although the gas stove may be put in slightly wider and bigger. With regards to the idea that Asians require a specific style around the house we say, 'no this is the traditional architecture of the UK'. We can adapt it and effectively that's been for more bedroom space. We adopt the principle of trying to get one bathroom between two rooms and not just for Asians but for everybody.

Through our housing officers we've tried to ensure that those who live in Ashram properties are not isolated within Ashram. Even though it's a predominantly BME facility we would ensure that they retain their gardens and we help them through our partnership work with Accord because we have a Groundworks Team. We realise if they don't look after their gardens

Ashram Angels in May 2006.

it's going to cause a tension, so we go out and do it and try to explain that they should do it and if they can't do it we help them. And we try and encourage our tenants to be good citizens in the locality.

The criteria for our tenants is largely the traditional one, they have to be on the housing list of the local authority and want to live in the housing where we have a house. They are, by and large, from the housing departments of the local authority so we cannot per se take somebody off the street.

A Strategic Alliance

We did have a difficult financial moment; we wanted to grow incrementally but because of the financial constraint we weren't going to be able to grow. We were smart enough to realise that if we didn't do anything we would wash away and the perception would be 'here is another BME with a five-year life and as the money dried up they couldn't sustain it'. The Board was such that of nine members six were Asian, including Hindu, Muslim and Sikh, and three of them were English. So we had a good mix.

And when the crunch came there was wisdom round the board table to say, 'actually if we are to survive three years down the line the best route for us would be to become part of a bigger organisation'. We recognised that growing for us meant growing with other partners; it wasn't growing ourselves because we were not capable at that level to become an independent developer/landowner.

So we focused on service provision and rather than have fifteen development partnerships we thought, 'why don't we have one?' That way we are driving efficiency and we are focusing on customer service delivery rather than spending a lot of time on trying to acquire land and build four houses here and six houses there.

We had to choose a partner that's going to allow us to continue retaining our brand and our ethos and our original principles of why we set out; a partner that will give us the freedom and the flexibility to operate the way we want to but then give us the comfort of a bigger organisation.

We very quickly realised that it wasn't going to be a takeover or a merger, it was going to be a strategic alliance. I was smart enough to realise that a strategic alliance eventually means giving away a lot of your control and freedom but you retain your integrity and your original objectives.

There were all sorts of tensions as you would expect. Some people said, 'you're abdicating, you've gone away' but there were two or three of us that said, 'yes but let's go and look at what our original ambition for this initiative was. It was basically to help our community as was then to look after its elderly.'

As things got tough and people became more economical in their ambition, then the care of the elderly and the frail was always going to become a tension point within the Asian family environment. So what we were doing was providing a potential solution for them to get their parents into another environment and get them looked after there. We said 'if that is our ambition to provide an outlet for people with elderly parents and to give them a guarantee of a good quality of service and to be sensitive to their cultural needs – as long as we can get that under the umbrella of another organisation and we can retain our identity then those are the key things for us.'

We were not there to build an empire with thousands of houses and fourteen different care schemes spread from Glasgow all the way to London. That wasn't our ambition and that wasn't deliverable. So we put forward a prospectus effectively saying, 'we are where we are and we're looking for a partner to go home with as it were'.

In the end, through a long drawn-out process, we selected Accord as our preferred partner – not because they were offering us any sweeteners or anything but because the strength of the argument was their understanding of our cultural needs, their understanding of us wanting to retain our identity. They wanted us to retain our identity because we would help them grow as well and there was a synergy there.

And we knew we needed to understand what's in it for the organisation that wanted the brand and the name to be within their stable. It was up to us then to exploit that relationship for the advantage of both sides in a positive way. So we joined up with Accord in 2003.

Since the merger with Accord, Ashram has grown. We were about 350 units and we've gone up to about 1,300 units. Over a five year period that's good, and we now have three residential homes caring for about 120 people. At the moment they are largely dependent upon social benefits but increasingly with Accord we are looking at schemes where they can be opened up to people who want to pay. We can do that because we have the financial resources and backing of Accord.

Enjoying a community day at Bosworth Drive.

The other thing we are able to do more cleverly is around the fact that not everybody needs to come into a care home or a sheltered home; so the thinking is 'why don't we provide them with care and support in their children's home if there is capacity to do that. The wife doesn't necessarily have to look after the parents. That means one of them doesn't have to give up their job to look after an elderly parent because we will take over the responsibility of providing care and support in the home environment.'

There is an interesting model going forward for giving care and support to people in their own home. A lot of the elderly folk we're looking after are coming out of houses with substantial equity. So they are saying, 'we don't want to go into a care home, we want to downsize and we want the care and support to be delivered to us'. So we are watching to see how our trends change.

That approach would be available to everyone. It's amazing we don't talk about, 'oh is the resident a Muslim where can we get a Muslim care worker?' We can actually now send an English lady or a gentleman to that home because we've trained them to be sensitive – and the residents are saying, 'I like her because she looks after me better, she understands me better'. It isn't about colour. Training is important as is taking time to help people to understand the cultural differences – and people respond to that approach. There is a lot of on-going training and we pride ourselves on that.

Community Action

Importantly after the merger with Accord, Ashram also raised the game in terms of service delivery to our tenants and we're also influencing a bigger agenda using all the capabilities that Accord has exposed to our benefit. So we've had initiatives like Bend it Like Birmingham, which is harnessing sport as a medium of communication to drive some cohesion within the local communities.

We've taken sports back to some of the tension points in communities and said 'let's focus on getting a good football team. Let's play together.' Suddenly black and white, Asian – it doesn't matter if you play a good game of football.

What we did cleverly was this – we sent the signal out into the community that we were not just a housing association. We were also acting as a local community base for organisations that were bringing about change in the localities where we were. So we were quite happy to take on some issues and to play them back into the local environment agenda or to central government.

We took some of the issues around forced marriages, some taboos around education, some taboos around Asians entering the world of sport.

We took on some big agendas and played them and amplified them at a local level and back at central government. We embraced the cultures and the diversities of the communities we serve today.

So we sponsor things like the film 'Land Gold Women', focusing on forced marriages and set in Birmingham. We amplified the situation within the community and when the film was in the production stage we lobbied for its funding, and then we opened up the market place for it. When the film was produced we sponsored its viewing.

By that time we were in the Accord Group so we used Accord's communications to say 'this is a taboo but we are brave enough to say we need to listen to this and try and change the mind-set'. We played it to the PCT, we played it to the health sector, and we played it to the police. It was precursor to some of the bigger debates.

Increasingly we are saying our role is to amplify the issues and bring those to the mainstream to try and influence the mainstream's thought process and service delivery. As an organisation we are never going to be

Ribbon Court is an extra-care sheltered housing scheme in Coventry with 50 one and two-bedroom apartments for people aged over 55. Built in 2009, Ribbon Court offers a diverse range of services, from providing self-contained homes to support and care to tenants when required.

able to meet the needs of our entire community and there is no ambition to move beyond Birmingham and our roots. But as part of our journey, a little bit of our own experiences came to light.

We have three very good schemes primarily for domestic violence and we've had national recognition. So far we haven't had an issue where we've had a break-in or the family create a scene on the doorstep. We are happy to talk with the family and say we are not going to interfere with the issues but we need to provide a residence because we are duty-bound to do it.

One of our schemes is a fifteen-bedroomed unit with an annexe where we can accommodate about twenty women. We provide discreetness, we provide protection from potential threat. We make sure that we are played into the statutory services and that the various people that are within our care have access to the best possible level of care possible. We provide all the creature comforts that the person could expect. We provide accommodation for the children as well.

Housing and AddVentures

What we are now doing in Accord as a group, and not just for Ashram, is that we are spending a lot of time trying to develop and devise schemes which are based around employment and training. If you look at Accord we have about 11,000 properties; that converts into roughly 40,000 tenants. They're all within inner-city locations, and in many cases difficult locations, where deprivation is rife and where the communities could break down – and then, if we're not careful, about it we could have the social tensions we have seen recently.

We have a significant role to play as a housing association and within that 40,000 tenants there will be 15-20% aged sixteen to twenty. What are we the housing association doing to help them get on to the employment market? And of course there is a self interest in the organisation to do that because if our tenant base is better off, if they get into the habit of going out to work and getting a new skill they will suddenly become proud of themselves and more confident. And suddenly they will say 'right I don't like that anti-social behaviour' and so they will look after the asset, the home, which is our self-interest. The less repair and maintenance we have to do, the better.

We have to do something positive. In our business plan we have three big strands now. Nearly 40-45% is housing, the traditional housing association model; 30-35% is care and support because we acknowledge we have to think about a new delivery model because the demographics are changing, people are getting older and care homes are quite expensive so we have to

A poster signed by the cast of 'Land Gold Women'. Left to right is Ghulam Shabar, Chair of Ashram Board with Akshay Parikh, Chair of Accord Group Board.

provide a different solution, we have to provide care at home rather than care in an institution.

And our third big strand is what we call AddVentures. This is Accord playing a very strong catalytic role to bring into our group some initiatives that are nationally driven and which we can then customise for our residents and the residents that live within our communities so that they become more economically active. That could be through volunteering, up-skilling, mentoring or getting people ready for self-employment.

Some of the residents we have are going to be very difficult to employ by somebody else, so our thinking is 'why don't we begin to employ them and when we've got them to a level they can move out. Things like ground maintenance, electrical work, plumbing, decorating – why don't we train people using our own procurement muscle.' We haven't cracked it but we have the ambition. That means we are not looking at it as a black and white issue.

As for Ashram, not everyone probably appreciates how difficult it was to get where we are but looking back it has provided a solution for our residents. And I think what Ashram will be remembered for is its contribution to making people understand the needs of a particular segment of the population and then amplify this in a positive way rather than just play on the BME card that we are being discriminated against.

We never use that word, because we believe it's not that, it's about breaking that gap of understanding between those who are policy makers and those who are in need of a service. Our role is not just to shout from the top of the rooftop about a particular bandwagon; our job is to try and understand the two mind-sets, and try and bridge that gap and effectively achieve a solution – and often it's a compromise solution.

We have won a lot of awards for the work we've done and Ashram is the only housing association in the country ever to win the UK Housing Association top award and HC Gold Award in the same year. We won the national category for delivering culturally sensitive support solutions and we also won the overall award for 'Outstanding Achievement' for England at the UK Housing Awards. They were in 2007 and were presented by the Chartered Institute of Housing and *Inside Housing* magazine. That double award was for Ashram's ground-breaking work to tackle the hidden problem of domestic violence within the Asian community.

Part of that recognition is that we're working differently and our delivery prompts things. The other key thing is credibility and trust. Apart from those schemes that are transient schemes, residents do stay with us for a long period of time.

Chapter 7

A COMMITTED ORGANISATION: FRY HOUSING TRUST

Rob Donath, Chief Executive

No Exclusion

I worked for twenty tears in financial services for a building society, which I thoroughly enjoyed. Then I found that the emphasis changed from mutuality to a very much more commercial approach. I took the opportunity to completely change my career and I went and worked for the Probation Service for about three years. This was the first time I came across Fry Housing Trust and I became very interested in their work. I was headhunted by the Trust to come and work with them as Housing Director and then was appointed Chief Executive in April 2007.

I found that Fry Housing Trust was a fantastically committed organisation, and the staff members were so keen to help. They were not do-gooders but they were committed to giving more opportunities to people who are more vulnerable and who have had a more difficult upbringing and life – and to help them through. They're keen to give people opportunities and support them and essentially make communities safer; that's what we do.

The Margery Fry Trust started in 1959. It was set up in memory of Margery Fry, who was a social justice campaigner all her life. She was quite a remarkable woman and was one of the first female magistrates in the UK. She

A young Margery Fry.

came from a Quaker family and she became interested in social justice in the First World War because a number of Quakers who were conscientious objectors were imprisoned. As a result the state of English prisons became much more public and the upper middle-class became much more interested in them.

Margery Fry took a firm interest and she became one of those responsible for setting up the Howard League for Penal Reform. She wrote a number of books, became a personality and appeared on the 'Brains Trust' on television, and supported a lot of good work. Again I think it's important to state that she wasn't a "do-gooder", she just thought that prison didn't work. I still believe that that is the case today.

So in 1959, a year after she died, a group of like-minded people set up an organisation called the Margery Fry Memorial Trust. They clubbed together and managed to get some public subscriptions to buy their first property in Moseley in Birmingham. It was a hostel for men who had come out of prison and it had a warden and his wife in it. I think it's fair to say they were quite paternalistic in their approach and I suppose they were a little bit too supportive so that often people would stay a bit longer than needed because they were quite institutionalised. I don't think there was quite the drive to get them to independence as the Trust has today.

The project was very much supported by the local community. Local councillors, the Probation Service, and the Police were all very pleased because it met the need of people coming out of prison that were homeless and coming out of the prison gates with nothing. Nowadays they leave with a plastic bag with underwear and a pair of trainers, about forty pounds in their pocket and with nowhere to go or, no support networks. This is a very unsatisfactory situation and has resulted in very high levels of re-offending

There's never been any great investment in this work so provision has traditionally developed through buying and converting large family homes. We provide short-term accommodation to

Margery Fry in later life.

120

help homeless people get back on their feet. The average stay with us is about six months. It does vary though, it can be two months or it can be eighteen months, depending upon their individual need. The barriers that offenders face when coming out are quite overwhelming, but homelessness is particularly significant.

Often when people go into prison it is the result of a quite chaotic lifestyle which could be unsettled family arrangements or it could be drugs, or mental health which is a huge issue – 70% of all offenders in prison have some sort of mental health issue. There's a physical health issue as well. If you've been in prison for about five years your physical age is about ten years older than if you'd been working in the community.

There are two ways people are referred to Fry Housing Trust. One could be that a prison resettlement team will identify if someone's not got a home to go to before release. That's the ideal way and it allows time for planning. We then identify if the person has additional needs, besides homelessness. A person might have mental health problems or drugs or alcohol issues and so a personalised package will be devised. There will be a pre-release plan, in which case either the probation officer or the prison will contact us and give us a lot of information, which we insist on to carry out a risk assessment.

We do not provide direct access housing. We don't just say, 'yes, send them along'. We carry out a very careful risk assessment. We look at the individual's needs; we look at what support we can give; we also look at the local community and we look at our current client group in each particular property. So, for instance, we wouldn't put too many individuals with similar needs together.

I suppose the unique part about the Trust is that we have a "no exclusion policy"; that means we will consider every referral thoroughly. It doesn't mean we will accept everybody, but we haven't got a blanket exclusion policy either. Some organisations will exclude arsonists, violent, or high risk offenders – they are very difficult to place. We don't exclude automatically. We look at what we can do, see how we can work together with that person and make a considered decision.

Working with Communities and Individuals

Initially the focus from Fry Housing Trust was completely on the individual and that's where we have changed over the years. Now the focus is much more balanced on the needs of the community. It's not a matter of just supporting people, it's about developing people and developing opportunities for them.

Criminality usually starts in childhood. Stereotypically our future clients will have had a single parent and they would start to truant at school. They may have somebody in their family who's a criminal. They may experiment with drugs or alcohol quite early on. They may have a lack of good peers and mentors. Essentially people entering the criminal justice system at about fifteen are very likely to become our clients when they reach adulthood. I think this is something that's only now being appreciated by politicians – that actually we need to identify people quite early on. It is possible to identify potential offenders when they are very young. The current 'Troubled Families' initiatives that the Government are working on to introduce, recognises that the prevention bit is far more important.

The Trust is working to keep communities safe by reducing re-offending but the demand for our services is huge. In 1959 the prison population was 30,000; it's now 86,000 and predicted to be about 96,000 in about five years' time.

The draft constitution of the Birmingham and West Midlands Discharged Prisoners' Aid Society – which later became part of the Fry Housing Trust.

There isn't an increase in crime rates but our society's view of crime and our treatment of crime is much more punitive. It costs about £40,000 to keep somebody in prison. A small investment in preventative work would save the state a significant amount of money.

The Trust works very closely with local communities where our properties are located in the sense that we communicate with people and we respond to neighbours' comments. We don't advertise our properties as there is quite a degree of sensitivity over their location. We work closely with the local police particularly in respect of the very high risk offenders who will be managed through multi-agency public protection arrangements. This process is normally managed by the police who chair the multi-agency public protection panels who meet to discuss very high risk offenders.

These high risk individuals will be managed in a different way. A low risk offender will be managed by a single agency; that might be either the police or the probation service. The multi-agency protection panels will consist of probation, police, social services, and housing who will all come together to discuss an individual case.

We work very closely with the Police and we work very closely with the probation service who are all very supportive of our work, but we also work with local communities in the sense that we have neighbours everywhere. We manage the properties very carefully and robustly. I believe that this approach reflects the needs of our communities. In the past we might have been more tolerant of anti-social behaviour but we are now much stronger in managing it. All our properties are shared so it's important to make our other clients safe and to make the local community safe. We take direct action against anti-social behaviour, we won't ignore it or pretend it's not happening.

We would consider ourselves highly professional, well trained and with a clear view of our commitment to the communities – not just the individuals. We are all trying to work together and we are trying to share the responsibility with the individual to make a positive contribution to communities. Lots of the offenders want to do that, they haven't had the chance.

We're very interested at the moment in something called desistance, which is an up and coming theory that people stop offending when a certain set of circumstances come together. We're not sure what these circumstances are yet and actually they're probably different for everybody.

Our role is to support people and work with them. When they arrive we know a lot about them. We know what their needs are and we know how to signpost them. On the most fundamental level, if you think of the hierarchy of needs, we give people shelter, warmth and support. We help them get signed up with the welfare benefits so they're not going to be starving. They've got supported accommodation. We'll get them signed up to doctors and start to deal with that and we'll work with mental health services if that is needed.

We'll signpost the drug and alcohol services and we'll work with people with the intention that within a period of time we will get them moved into independent accommodation – and we'll also give them help with that. We

A drop in day at Coventry Fry Housing.

do floating support as well, which has several strands, but for people moving on we'll make sure they're ready and then help them resettle.

Preparing them for moving on is vital, especially with regards to self-esteem. Literacy and numeracy are crucial amongst our client group. For lots of people work is not even a possibility because they can't read or write, so we need to address that. We do some of that work ourselves, we do get some people in from external organisations and we also do signposting – so there's a range of ways to help. We're not drug experts and we're not mental health experts, for example, and so we work with people who are.

We support people into employment and we have a specialist employment worker and that's one of the things you really notice is that some people can be scared to write a CV, or scared to apply for anything. That's where we need to support them to give them that confidence.

In terms of self-esteem one of the best things we've got going is Fry Voices Together, our resident engagement group. It is a group of clients that come together from all around the Trust, from various schemes, and they can tell us what they think of us, what they think of our services, and they work with us to develop policies and procedures. They tell us what makes a good support worker and they drive a lot of what we do. My proudest moment was when our Fry Voices Together group won the Accord Group Residents' Team of the Year Award.

For some people that was the first time they'd won anything like that. It's fantastic. Many of them also ran the marathon last year. Again, they were so pleased because it was the first time some clients had done anything like that. We've got people in their thirties and forties who've not achieved anything or been praised for anything.

A Personalised Service

We've got about 30 properties across the West Midlands and they vary from properties that are staffed 24/7, to properties that are staffed 9-5 Monday to Friday, and to properties that we just provide visiting cover to. We provide about 200 bed spaces in Birmingham, Coventry, Solihull, Leamington, Bromsgrove, Sandwell and Nuneaton.

We provide a variety of properties in a range of areas often developed to meet local needs and they're developed with the probation service. For instance, a very high risk person or a very vulnerable person will go into a 24/7 property with fifteen or sixteen people with their own bedrooms and

Chapter House receives a makeover in 2011.

shared facilities but support available throughout. There'd be one member of staff during the night and three or four during the day.

Then we might step them down to day cover and then we might move them on to visiting cover. We get a lot of professional people that may become clients too, that actually aren't so vulnerable but they have lost their homes for all sorts of reasons, particularly now with internet offences. So they don't need that much support but being homeless is not something they're used to and so we help people not to be homeless and to deal with homelessness and move them on.

Each person would be assigned a key support worker who would take responsibility for that person because it's about building a relationship of trust. You can't keep chopping and changing the personnel because that's one thing that offenders will tell you – their probation officer's changed, the police they're dealing with change so there's no consistency. So we allocate our support worker, who will work with the person very early on and we produce a support plan.

That support plan identifies that person's needs from what they feel they need and also what the probation officers are telling us, because we get people telling us they haven't got a drugs problem but actually we know they have. We work with people to agree what they want out of their time with us. For some people that's quite a quick resettlement, for people who don't have so many support needs. We'll work with them, get them signed up, get them on to housing lists and to claim benefits.

The job centres have tightened up. In the past if you missed an appointment or went in late you would get another chance. Now your benefits are immediately stopped. For somebody whose only method of living has been offending, to stop their finance when we're trying to rehabilitate them is difficult. That's the Government's agenda. I'm not saying that's wrong I'm just observing that the impact is negative.

As soon as their Job Seekers Allowance gets suspended for two weeks then they have no money for that time and the housing benefit stops. So they start immediately to get into arrears with us and problems start building up – all the problems that we're trying to get away from.

We are a housing association and we get our funding from two places. We charge a rent and we get grants from the Supporting People programme. The probation service used to pay us to deliver the service but now it's Supporting People. That pays for the staff. We don't have a big turnover of staff because people love the organisation. We have about 70 staff, who are highly trained. They are trained in dealing with high-risk offenders, dual diagnosis where people have a mental health and a drugs issue, challenging behaviour and more. The training is continual and it reflects the changes as the criminal justice system changes.

That's what makes us different, that our staff are highly trained. There is a cost to that, that's reflected in our staff salaries although they're not high. But there's a danger because when a local authority comes to re-tender for the business somebody comes in who'll say they'll undercut our hourly rate by £5 and pay a minimum rate for a member of staff.

Roughly it probably costs £800 per week for someone to be in prison and it probably costs the country between £100 and £150 a week to keep them out of prison with a completely personalised service. That personalised service we provide is quite exceptional. You can find accommodation anywhere. In parts of Birmingham some big old houses have been taken over by landlords for ex-prisoners. They charge a high rent but the landlord will just say yes to anybody. There might be three arsonists in the same building; or have six high-risk offenders in there. It's very worrying that there's such inappropriate accommodation.

Two clients from the Coventry Scheme taking part in a regular activity to help them improve their cooking skills to help them when they move into independent accommodation.

Fry Housing Trust has about 200 bed spaces and we probably get 1,400-1,500 referrals a year. The demand for our services is unbelievable. In the past we did have people who were with us for three of four years, sometimes five years. Those people, who have many needs, probably couldn't be supported by us anymore because we're now contracted with the local authority, through the Supporting People Fund, to move people on between six and nine months.

What that does is to exclude the most needy people. If somebody has got significant needs we know we can't move them on. We also have great difficulty in moving high-risk offenders on. Obviously we have to be very careful and work with the multi-agency public protection panels.

Accord: A Family Approach

We started to talk to the Accord Group at the end of 2006. The reason for that was that we had a Chief Executive who was retiring and like all organisations in the voluntary sector we were threatened with funding cuts here, there and everywhere. We'd worked really well as a small organisation. We'd been quite nimble and able to innovate very quickly but we did recognise that we had restricted capacity to get the most out of it.

We recognised that we needed to support our infrastructure and we wrote to a number of big housing associations and the response was fantastic. Everybody wanted to work with us as we'd got a good reputation, which is fantastic, and we do something a bit different – we only work with offenders and we're really good at it.

We listened to what other organisations were telling us about how we could work together with them and we decided that the Accord Group offered a family approach. Our organisation would be allowed to continue to work with its specialism and be treated as an individual organisation within a group rather than be subsumed into a group. There was a commitment to keep the Fry Housing Trust brand and that was really important.

We were very pleased with the assurances we got from the Accord Group so we joined the Group formally in October 2007. We were welcomed aboard and the Housing Corporation, as it was then, was very supportive. We'd had to put a very good business case to the Housing Corporation and we had to talk with a lot of stakeholders – probation services, local authorities – and everybody said 'yes, it makes complete sense'.

We liked the culture of the Accord Group; it feels like an organisation that exists for local communities and for Midland societies. We liked that very much. We had talked to a national player and that Midlands bit would have disappeared and we felt we would have been absorbed. We are based in the Midlands and the Accord Group operates in the Midlands.

Since we joined the Accord Group our I.T. systems have improved tremendously and there is more scope for that. We've been able to share lots of experiences because we bring a much more focused support arrangement to the Accord Group. The Accord Group care and support is really good and well developed but it is in all directions – learning difficulties, dementia, the elderly and others. So we've learnt a lot from that and I think we've brought a lot to them, particularly in managing unpopular and challenging client groups.

We liked the fact that a lot of the Accord Group's business was dealing with vulnerable people. The ethos is there and there has been a synergy. We've come together and I think we've improved the Accord Group and they've improved us. We're still independent, we're working away doing our own things and innovating – and the Accord Group have been really supportive of that. Our world is changing very rapidly in terms of probation reform, prison reforms,

Clients taking part in a creative activity to design some art work to be displayed at their scheme.

privatisation of the prison system, and even the role of the police. We face some big challenges and I think we are really supported by the Accord Group.

There are very few organisations that just do what we do but it's interesting that similar organisation we used to work with have started to become competitors to us in this new world of the voluntary sector. Once we would have got together and shared things, now we're finding it a bit difficult because we're actually competing against each other for our own business.

We've lost that sort of stakeholder input and it can be a bit lonely but the Accord Group has stepped in to say 'yes come on we can help you with this, yes we can do that'. We've shared good practice and actually there are quite a lot of similarities between different vulnerable groups.

Making Communities Safer

One of the things you might come across is the Eden Alternative. That is about reducing the loneliness of an individual. It is designed for the elderly and it's about getting children to come into care homes or using animals to re-socialise people who've become very insular. Prisoners are exactly the same.

The prison experience is absolutely traumatic for lots of people and actually they shut off. Their only method of survival is to go back within themselves. They come out exactly like that. It's one of the reasons why shared accommodation is good because it re-socialises people and that's really important.

Our residents like to be called clients. We asked them. We probably work with four to five hundred people a year. In terms of success it's one of the most difficult things to assess. Our real success is to say 'right, we've got to make communities safer. We want to make individuals safer. We want to reduce re-offending.'

There are lots of different client groups within the criminal justice system. Some of the people we are dealing with provide quite a challenge. There is one called Prolific and Priority Offenders. These are the people that probably commit 80% of the crimes. They are about 10% of the offenders but they commit most of the crime. The police take a particular view of working with these people and we work with them a lot.

If we can stop somebody re-offending for three months they might re-offend again but actually that's the first three months that they've never re-offended in their adult life. So it's a fantastic outcome. We reckon that probably between 60% of our clients don't re-offend. The general re-offending rate depends on how long an offender has served but it's probably between 60 and 70%. We're getting re-offending down and making communities safer.

We don't judge people. Our staff will deal with people who've committed the most serious crimes but we don't judge. We work with the person, not the crime. We focus on individuals, we work with individuals and we try and give people opportunities to make a positive contribution to society. That's what we do. Some people aren't ready for it, some are but we help people wherever they are on their journey. We are a professional organisation that exists to help the community.

We are also looking to do a lot more prevention work. We recognise that we can't do much more than what we're doing in the sense that there's no more funding for it. We can't increase the accommodation although there's a desperate need for accommodation, but if we went anywhere and said we're going to open a building specifically for offenders we'd never get planning permission.

Essentially we've got what we've got and we've got to keep that, and the development over the last ten years has been floating support services. These are services that can be delivered into people's own properties; it's not based around our accommodation it's based around delivering a service into the community.

There isn't any more funding for that either so what we're looking at doing is trying to move in a little bit earlier by doing some work with troubled families, do some partnership work with mental health organisations, do some work with the prisons. Birmingham Prison is the first one to go private so we're doing some work with them. There's a new prison in Wolverhampton and we're doing some work with them.

We also are trying to work with younger people, where there's a huge gap. We need to divert them from the criminal justice system. If we put them in the system they become part of the system and they come out more vulnerable than when they went in.

What we do is to try and build a relationship that will be positive for both us and the individual but also for the community. That's what our staff are so skilled at. We are dealing with people who've had a poor deal of the cards in life. We are almost trying to shine the light and say it can be alright, it can work and for lots of people they've never lifted their eyes up to see out before.

Chapter 8

CARING AND HOUSING, LOCALLY: MOSELEY AND DISTRICT CHURCHES HOUSING ASSOCIATION

Starting a Housing Association
John Simmonite MBE, first Association Director

Not long after I came to Birmingham in 1960, I began to realise there was something I must do. But what was it? I enjoyed the work which had brought me to Birmingham but knew it had nothing to do with that. Although 'what' remained a mystery, 'where' seemed to be associated with Balsall Heath and North Moseley. The feeling was at its strongest, almost a sense of excitement, as I travelled through those roads on my way to or from the city centre.

I usually skip the advertisement pages of the *Evening Mail* but one day I noticed a small advert. A new organisation called the Balsall Heath Association wanted volunteers. Was this what I had been waiting for? I went along to find out.

The Balsall Heath Association had a property in Varna Road. It was in poor condition and the first need was to improve the building, to make it more attractive, somewhere local people could visit. Then one day I was asked to go out, knock on doors and say 'we are here, is there anything we can do to help you?'

It was time consuming work. Most of the large houses in neighbouring roads were multi-occupied. A family would have one room in which to live, eat and sleep. There were cookers on landings. Other facilities were shared. The majority of people I visited were families with young children and almost all were eager to talk. Housing was usually at the top of their list. Those who felt it pointless, a waste of time, I would urge to put their names down.

There were problems. The Balsall Heath Association could, and did, help people resolve (just as, happily, it continues today) but so often the difficulties we listened to stemmed from a total lack of adequate housing and there was little we could do about that.

One fine, warm summer evening, I was walking home thinking about the problems of a family I had just visited when I fell into step with Freddie Carpenter, then vicar of St. Mary's, Moseley. He was concerned about the housing conditions of some of his parishioners living in multi-occupied houses in Church Road and typically had visited them to see what he could do to help.

We arrived at the vicarage in School Road and continued talking for a long while. Eventually Freddie said, 'why don't we start a housing association?'

Staff and residents at the tenth anniversary party at Carpenter Place in 1996, with the Venerable F. C. Carpenter second from the right on the back row. A founder of the Association in 1966 and its first chairman, the scheme was named after him. All photographs are thanks to Esther Boyd.

In 1991 the Venerable F. C. Carpenter recalled that 'two things triggered off the start of the Association. A baby died in a damp basement flat in Church Road, where a young postman and his wife lived at an exorbitant rent paid to an absentee landlord. Then a woman whose husband was in prison began to be threatened by the "agent" of another landlord already notorious in the district. It was in the days of the Rachman-type scandals up and down the country. We had to do something.' (Moseley and District Churches Housing Association, 'Silver Jubilee Report', 1990-91).

Although I knew nothing about housing associations, if it meant being able to help solve housing problems, I was very much in favour of the idea. We agreed to meet again in I think, three weeks. During that time we would both seek others who might become useful members of a steering committee.

Helped by the British Churches Housing Trust, the steering committee moved gradually towards the formation of a housing association. Freddie was keen to involve the local Council of Churches and so we took our plans to a meeting of the Moseley and District Council of Churches, which at that time brought together the churches of Balsall Heath, Kings Heath and Moseley.

At that time I was the lay representative of my own church to the local Council of Churches and so present when the Moseley and District Council

Esther Boyd as Chair of the Association with Councillor Stan Austin, Chair of Birmingham City Council's Housing Committee, and Shaheed and Rahila Iqbal and their son, Umar. The Iqbals were the occupants of the Association's 1,000th tenancy in 1991.

The official opening of Silver Jubilee Villa in 1992. Left to right are Esther Boyd, Chair; Andrew Matheson, director of the Association; Dr Carl Chinn, community historian at the University of Birmingham; and Councillor Bernard Zissman. The house had been renovated from the Associations' Jubilee Fund, and the project was a work experience opportunity for building work trainees.

Jubilee Villa provided a home for three people who had been homeless and who had been living at the St Basil's centre, a hostel for the homeless. St Basil's continued to provide the three residents with support to help them re-establish themselves in the community, and the scheme helped other homeless people by freeing up three spaces at the hostel.

of Churches endorsed the proposal to start a housing association. So we started the Moseley and District Churches Housing Association in September 1966. Freddie was the obvious choice as Chairman of the Management Committee and it was a shock to the rest of us when, two years later, Freddie moved to Portsmouth. He took his experience with him and was involved in starting a housing association there, too.

At last, though, we could begin to do something. I shall never forget the time and effort involved in our first scheme, the purchase of 53 Mayfield Road and its conversion into three self-contained flats. We bought and converted other properties but progress was frustratingly slow. The only source of finance was 90% improvement loans from the City of Birmingham. We had to raise the other 10% before a loan could be approved. Most of that money came from members of local churches.

The Housing Act 1974 brought new controls and more money for housing associations. The Association was able to expand rapidly and I came under increasing pressure to devote even more of my time to its work. It was not an easy decision to make but with family support I gave up my day job and moved into the office we opened above the West Bromwich Building Society in Moseley Village. I never had cause to regret the decision. There was so much to do. Other

The official opening of Auckland Road in Sparkbrook by Sir Christopher Benson (front left) then Chairman of the Housing Corporation. In the middle at the front is Stuart Chapman with his mother and on the right is Councillor Bert Carless, deputy chairman of Birmingham City Council's Housing Committee.

The project was a small cul-de-sac of houses built on previously derelict land. The house that Stuart and his mother moved into was especially adapted so that there were 'no impediments to his enjoyment of a full and independent life'.

housing associations were also growing quickly and by the end of the 1970s it seemed that the housing need was being met and waiting lists were falling.

It is good to meet others who were involved at the start. People like the late Margaret Brown, who became secretary at the same time as I was asked to be chairman when Freddie Carpenter left Birmingham in 1968. Margaret's legal knowledge and contacts were invaluable to the Association. And Patty MacGregor who, when the steering group first met, knew more about housing associations than the rest of us put together, because she worked for one. Patty became the Association's first housing manager and her influence in shaping management policies is still at the heart of the Association.

Others who shared the responsibilities of those early days were Miss J. M. Armstrong, E. J. Attenborough, David Gould, John Humby, Dr N. G. Lambert, Elizabeth Lawson, Rev. Peter Lewis, Rev. Trevor Rowe and, not to be left out, our first employee, David Thomas.

(These memories of John Simmonite MBE are compiled mostly from an interview in *Birmingham 13*, circa 1996. I am grateful to John Northam the editor of *Moseley B13 Magazine* for permission to include this interview. There is also some material from the 'Annual Review' Moseley & District Churches Housing Association, 1996; and the 'Annual Review' Moseley & District Churches Housing Association, 2002/2003).

Empowering Tenants
Esther Boyd

We bought our house in Queenwood Road in north Moseley in 1972. I was an architect working in Edgbaston and I was giving up work to have a family. I wanted to be living in an area which was lively and where I could contribute while I was at home – not doing paid work I could do things in the community. We then met Margaret Selby, who was running The Lane Neighbourhood Advice Centre, set up by Christian Aid I think, on the Ladypool Road in Sparkbrook.

We had heard her talk at a meeting about how important it was for middle-class people to move back into this sort of area because middle-class people were moving away. So Howard and I decided to buy this house, which in 1972 cost us £3,750 because the area was 'red-lined' as a bad investment area. Luckily, we could afford to buy it with a short-term bank loan as we couldn't get a mortgage. That's how I came into the area.

I then became the community architect to a group in Saltley: St Joseph's and St Saviour's Youth and Community Association. They didn't need both churches and they had decided to convert one of them into community use and I was the community architect for them. As I wasn't in practice (I had taken a career break and had three young children) I had no professional insurance. I took the job to a small practice in Edgbaston and I was employed by them to do the work. I didn't feel that I should take professional responsibility on my own.

A probation officer who was a member both of the Saltley committee and the Moseley and District committee suggested that I be invited on to the M&D committee and I joined in 1979. I'm a Quaker and we believe that our faith should lead to action in the community, trying to make the world a better place for everyone. I realised that M&D was working hard to improve housing conditions for people in greatest need – I knew this as we lived in a street with several M&D properties – and we still do.

The presentations at the 1994 Annual General Meeting to Nagin Palmer of the Ashram Housing Association (second from the left at the front); Mr and Mrs Gardener from Runcorn Road at the back; and representatives from the United Churches Housing Association on the right.

The Association had been started in 1966 by local professionals who were churchgoers and they included an accountant, John Simmonite, who became the first director; an architect, John Humby; a clergyman, Freddie Carpenter (Carpenter Place in Oldfield Road is named after him); a doctor, Frank Alexander; a lawyer, Francis Allen; a teacher, David Swinfen; and a surveyor: David Gould.

M&D was managed by local professionals working for the community and they did get paid. It wasn't much but they did get paid for designing things, for estate agency and that kind of thing. Later, the Housing Act 1974 brought in new controls so that you couldn't do professional work for a housing association and get paid for it if you were on the committee of management – the legislation also brought in more income for housing association developments.

When I joined the committee, M&D was a small organisation. It was still managed by professionals who were part of the community, but they were now unpaid. David Swinfen was chair until he became Head of Moseley School; Francis Allen then took over as chair; Frank Alexander remained on the committee. John Humby and David Gould worked as paid consultants.

The very first offices were above David Gould's offices in St Mary's Row. Then we moved to an office that was opposite the 'Fighting Cocks', above what is now a betting shop. There were two parking spaces, accessed from King Edward Road, for the use of consultants and visitors. All staff and committee members lived within walking distance from the office, as did all our tenants.

Visualising the office then there was John Simmonite as director, somebody dealing with housing management and somebody dealing with development. At one stage we even had a part-time architect working from that office, and there were housing officers.

The name of the Association is Moseley and District Churches Housing Association; it was set up by local Christians and was managed with a Christian ethos – though I personally dislike the use of the adjective "Christian" when the meaning it implies is "good". My mother was Jewish and I was taught from a very young age not to use the word Christian when I meant ethical, because so-called Christian virtues are not the monopoly of Christians. People of all faiths, and of no religious faith, are good citizens and work hard to make the world a better place for everyone.

So yes; the Association was Christian but as far as our tenants were concerned, it was an organisation for people in housing need. There has never, ever been any selection of tenants on anything other than housing need.

It was a very hands-on organisation. We looked at every single application and discussed whether that person was the sort of person who really needed housing by M&D. So if they earned over £100 a week or if they owned a car they weren't the sort of people we needed to house. We needed to house those in the greatest housing need. There was a trickle of applicants compared to what things are like now and we went through everything in great detail.

In those days you received the total development cost from the Government; HAG, as it was called – Housing Association Grant. You did not have to borrow so we were free from borrowing risk, and also from borrowing costs. The rents could be affordable.

In 1980, a year after I joined, I prepared a plan that showed all the properties in our ownership. It was quite interesting that I was asked not to make it public beyond the committee because it was thought that people shouldn't know exactly which houses were Moseley and District houses. There were very few new builds. It was on the whole a matter of making the existing homes into decent homes.

The Management Committee was still very white, middle-class and Christian. I once suggested that an environmental health officer I knew might be asked to join the Committee. After a long silence somebody who knew him said quietly, 'but he is

The official opening in 1995 of St Bede's, Kings Heath with Nick Raynsford MP, the shadow housing minister (front); Councillor Theresa Stewart (in blue); and Esther Boyd, Chair of the Association. On the right is the Bishop of Birmingham, Mark Santer; behind him is Andrew Hargreaves, MP for Hall Green, with the moustache; and Glen von Malachowski, assistant director SENSE.

St Bede's was an integrated scheme of self-contained accommodation for people with different needs. Seven of the seventeen flats were for people with sensory impairments and were to be managed by the charity SENSE. Four flats were for people with learning disabilities and six more were for those with general housing needs.

Jewish'. That made me feel terribly uncomfortable because my mother was Jewish so I am Jewish, as Jewishness follows through the maternal line. I quickly said to them 'I think I am here under false pretences. Didn't you realise that I am Jewish?' There was embarrassment but they didn't ask me to leave.

The relationships between committee members, staff and tenants were very formal and, for me, difficult to accept. Committee members could only exchange ideas with the Director – staff never attended meetings of the Management Committee (and there were no other meetings) and tenants were treated in a very paternalistic way. We acted in their best interests, according to our judgment. There was no direct connection with tenants and there was absolutely no input from tenants and also no involvement by the committee with members of staff.

It was when Andrew Matheson was the Director that he started the idea of having an annual garden party by inviting the tenants in to what were then the new offices in Alcester Road. That was a chance to get to know people, although living with tenants all around me in Queenswood Road I already knew quite a lot of tenants because they were my neighbours.

In my time as Chair from 1990, I was keen to begin work towards the empowerment of tenants. This was encouraged by Andrew Matheson and welcomed by our tenants. And it all started at one of the garden parties when I talked with a tenant called Pat Faulkner, who is still a tenant. She had come along to the garden party thinking what could she do and through talking to Pat, we had the joint idea of more tenant involvement.

I thought that Pat would be a very useful person on a committee of tenants and so I asked her would she be willing to help me, as chair, in setting up such a committee and getting more tenants' involvement. So we worked together on that and have remained good friends. A Service Users Committee was set up, which I chaired until Pat felt able to take over.

Tenants were later given the opportunity to elect two board members and Pat and Ann Delaney became tenant members of the Board. The tenants' representatives were not there because they were experts in X, Y or Z – they were people who were there because they had experience of being tenants; purely and simply for that reason.

So we had tenants on the Committee and we also brought people on to what was now the Board from the community who had other skills and who were, like the tenants, close to the community. The Board itself concentrated on governance issues but with the increase in work and development we set up various committees to work with staff on operational issues – and not all of the people on those committees were board members. We could bring on

Members of the Moseley Community Co-operative moving into their homes in Louis Lorne Road, Moseley in 1995. This was a management co-operative set up by tenants of the Association to run the housing.

people from outside. The main committees were development, finance, housing management and tenants.

In this way the Board and committees became very diverse. Andrew Matheson said at one stage that we had so many people from black and minority ethnic communities on our Board that technically we could count as a BME organisation. To me it was a really important thing to make the organisation more representative of the community but it was also important to have tenants having a proper voice.

After I became chair, the principal financial challenge was the change from direct funding from the taxpayer, via the Housing Corporation, towards majority funding from the money market. We had to change ourselves, to change the way the Association was organised, to meet that challenge – but we could now invest more and be more effective.

In the six years I was chair the Association doubled in size. We had been asked to take over Newhaven Housing Association back in 1984. It was a local, small, non-charitable HA which had properties in our core district and also in Edgbaston. This was our first venture outside Moseley and Balsall Heath but the Balsall Heath Housing Co-operative was our first management contract in the early 1990s.

Many houses which we had subdivided into flats were now de-converted into large family houses, reflecting the changed needs of our diverse

The official opening of the office/reception extension at the Association's Alcester Road offices in 1996. In the forefront is Pat Faulkner, one of the first tenants involved in the Association's Board.

community. The move from providing housing for local people in greatest housing need, with a very local base, to working with tenants and other members of the community to deliver the best possible service for a slightly wider area, was significant. No longer do all tenants live within pram pushing distance from the office, but the Association retains a strong local focus.

Sue Wainwright, a local welfare rights researcher (amongst other things) followed me as Chair; she was followed by Martin Robertson who preceded Douglas McCarrick. We recognised that we must provide homes, not houses. Not just shelter to keep people dry and warm, but also homes which provide

The official on-site start of the redevelopment of the former Beverley Hotel on the Stratford Road in Sparkbrook in 1995. Andrew Matheson, the Association's Director is back left. In front of him is Councillor Doug McCarrick, later a chair of the Association, and Esther Boyd, then Chair. At the front is Nagin Palmer and behind him is Jay Chauhan, both of whom were representing the Ashram Housing Association. The group is made up by Heather Mytton, Regional Director of the Housing Association.

security, a place to develop friendships and relationships and where people can lead fulfilling lives.

Working with our tenants, sometimes with the help of their mentors, we improved our understanding of the particular needs of different sections of our diverse community and strove to meet them. Our identity was 'Caring and Housing, locally'.

In 2004 on the surface all seemed good: the accounts balanced and the last monitoring report from Birmingham City Council Housing Department was favourable. We felt that we were doing a good job.

Clearly, however, the Board's governance wasn't good enough. It appears that there were things under the surface we were not aware of. In 2005, the Audit Commission's report for the Housing Corporation told the Board that the situation was serious and that is why we had to move on and eventually became part of the Accord Group in 2009.

It was a shock to us and for a long time we lived in denial, I must confess. Some of the Report focused on tenant participation as a problem and we could not see how that could be. Then the cost of putting us into special measures combined with cost of the repairs caused by the tornado in 2005 meant that the Association got into severe financial difficulties. If the two hadn't happened together it could have been different. The tornado was devastating as so much of our property was in its path.

I left the Board in 2007 after 28 years. I am still a member of the Association, which means that I am now a member of Accord. I am pleased that M&D is still accountable to the diverse, local communities of Moseley and its neighbouring districts.

Joining Accord
David Cusack, chief executive 2006-2011

When I arrived in 2006 we had twelve months to prepare for when the Audit Commission came back to re-inspect us. In that twelve months we had to do an awful lot of work; we had to overhaul a number of our policies, such as our repairs policy, our ASB policy, allocations and so on, we then had to re-train staff in the changes and work with them to change the culture to a 'can do' organisation. We had to produce a whole suite of new information leaflets, working with staff and tenants that clearly told tenants what to expect from M&D.

We came through and in May 2007 we were really pleased with the one star, given the length of time we had to prepare and the scale of the task we faced. That was followed up in October by the Housing Corporation taking us out of supervision. They were satisfied we'd turned a corner.

Esther Boyd, Chair of the Association, making a speech at the official opening of the Stratford Road development in 1996. This was just before the tape was cut by Councillor Mike Nangle, Chair of Birmingham City Council's Urban Renewal Committee (hands clasped in front of him), and Heather Mytton, Regional Director of the Housing Association.

The formerly dilapidated Beverley Hotel had been turned into family accommodation in a joint project with the Ashram Housing Association. At a cost of £752,000 it now consisted of eight houses for large families needing four or six bedrooms.

It's been a roller coaster two years and we have known for some time that we needed to work in partnership with another successful and established organisation to help us move forward. We are really pleased to be joining the Accord Group, which has a track record of high performance and putting residents at the heart of everything it does.

M&D will remain committed to the south of Birmingham but will, over the next few years, develop and improve services and we believe increase the number of homes we manage. This is a momentous day in M&D's 41 year history and the start of an exciting new journey.

We were able to deliver the Government's Decent Homes, but this is quite a minimum standard, and what we want are homes that are fit for the future and we were struggling financially to achieve that. The Accord Group are supporting M&D financially so that we can do the work we know is needed to residents' homes. From a tenant perspective that's fantastic, but it's not just about that. M&D will maintain its identity and its independence, as well as its local community focus, but it will also be able to draw upon the expertise of fellow group members.

On top of that, we will be using the Group's financial management resources and we will be buying into its IT support, so that all the back-room services that keep an organisation going will be handled for us by the Group. This will leave us to concentrate on improving the services and managing our homes in the most efficient way.

(This account by David Cusack of the period 2006-2008 is taken from press releases in 2008 about M&D joining the Accord Group.)

The Future for Moseley and District
Sara Woodall

I joined M&D in December 2011 as Interim Chief Executive, although I have worked for the Accord Group for nearly thirteen years. I was originally part of the team that worked with M&D just before and during the time it joined the Group, so I knew many of the staff, residents and board members and from my first day in the office I was warmly welcomed by all.

We all had great plans for M&D to really cement its place as a leader in neighbourhood and community engagement and management; but to ensure that its future was secure, to deliver on our aspirations and strengthen our offer to the communities of Birmingham, the M&D board as well as the Accord Group Board took the decision that we would go through a legal process to Transfer the Engagements of M&D into Accord to give M&D a really sound financial footing. This happened at the end of April 2012 after a period of extensive consultation with customers, staff and stakeholders.

In this period of massive change for housing and communities our ambitions now are simple but adventurous and will leave us poised on the edge of a new future. We will still keep at our heart our aspirations around excellent service, engaging with residents, the importance of neighbourhoods and communities and the need to invest and grow.

We believe that our work today is more important than ever before. The Localism Act will shift power away significantly from central to local government and we must make sure that third sector organisations such as M&D contribute fully to this agenda for the benefit of our communities.

We have a huge opportunity to support our customers to help them become active citizens and to participate in the decisions that affect them and their neighbourhoods. With the communities in Moseley, Balsall Heath, Kings Heath and Edgbaston though, we are not starting with a blank sheet of paper. Many of those living in these neighbourhoods are already active in lots of ways and part of our role is to work with our local community partners to ensure more joined up thinking and doing.

Our plans for the future include making sure that we adapt to local needs and respond to tackling joblessness. With unemployment at the highest level for seventeen years, we are encouraging our service users who want to learn new skills to access volunteer opportunities both inside and outside the Accord Group. In this way they will be able to increase their employment opportunities. We are also working closely with Caldmore to make sure that within the Accord Group all volunteer experiences are positive ones.

Residents cut the cake for the future of M&D at the 2012 Garden Party.

Our commitment to develop and deliver services in line with the personalisation agenda will be continued. We focus on delivering quality services to residents living in our schemes but we have broadened accessibility to our support services through our working with Ashram in delivering a 'Taste 4 Life' service,

There is much more exciting work ahead. We want to work further with schools and colleges, including another exciting project with the Challenge initiative; we want to work more closely with our partners to deliver learning disabilities and young people support services; and we will work more with resident scrutiny and co-regulation.

It is important to stress that we are as committed as ever to remaining one of the top performing community housing associations in the Birmingham area and to provide excellent homes and services for the communities we serve.

Tenant Engagement
John Gorman

Tenant engagement has made a big impact. I have been on the Moseley and District Churches Housing Association Tenants' Forum since at least 1997. As tenants we gained new skills and experiences and helped improve services. We identified priorities and future tasks, were in touch with management and Board representatives and attended various meetings. Because of that we were influencing decisions.

Through the involvement of residents we came to realise the benefits of working together, and so encouraged others to come together and be involved. M&D has supported and promoted the involvement of tenants for a good many years. It is vital for fairness, equality and value for money for residents to have a voice in the shaping of the services of the Association and for staff and residents to work together and hold contractors to account as well as the Association.

This process is carried out through forum service users, steering groups, armchair audits, surveys, questionnaires, estate walkabouts, scheme meetings, general meetings, and conferences. There are also various training opportunities for residents and a Resident Editorial Panel quarterly and a Resident Scrutiny Panel. There is also a Group-wide panel Resident Inspector Project underway.

Chapter 9

A PERSONAL JOURNEY: CALDMORE HOUSING ASSOCIATION

Barrie Blower MBE

A Formidable Force: Caldmore Residents Action Group

Community has always been important to me. Perhaps my origins gave me the motivation to play my part in the Caldmore Housing story. From 1943 to 1976 I lived in Caldmore in Walsall with my parents. My father was a train driver at Bescot and mum was a metal polisher. I finished my education at fifteen and dad invited me to work with him on the railway. I had been expelled twice, first from the local grammar school followed by a short stay at a secondary high school as I was not very academic. After a year on the railway a job I disliked immensely, I went to look for something else. I went to the labour exchange and saw the posters up for the Navy, Army and Air Force and seeing a ship entering New York harbour on the Navy poster, I thought 'that'll do me'.

I was sixteen and they asked me 'can you swim, tie knots or has anyone in your family been in the Navy?' I said no. I was told I could join but would need my parents' permission to do so. I went in as a stoker in 1956 and came out as a stoker eleven years later, still unable to swim. In a sense the Navy was my community for over a decade.

On my release I was sent to a colonel in Wolverhampton who placed people into jobs when they left the forces. He got me into the power station at Wolverhampton as a stoker and I was pretty hopeless. Having joined the electricians' union I became a shop steward as I'd been a bit of an organiser during my time in the navy as the stokers' welfare representative. When I visited the ash pits and saw those old men pulling out hot clinker wearing just flimsy masks and torn gloves I was very upset and this was my first challenge. Over a five year period I was sacked several times for acting on behalf of the workers. In fact every time I went in to see the gaffer he would sack me but I'd be reinstated shortly afterwards.

In the meantime the house we lived in was privately rented in Caldmore and couldn't be improved without the landlord's permission. The houses were mainly privately rented with outside toilets and no bathroom but they were structurally sound. Tenants maintained them and kept them to a good standard of decoration but they were very much in need of major improvements. However, the area had been blighted by a council report which had recommended widespread clearance so landlords were not prepared to invest in the properties.

We lived at 29 Victor Street in the heart of Caldmore. We were lucky as my mum, dad, me and my brother were lodging in a house in Leamore until 1943 with my uncle and aunt but then my uncle's mother was taken seriously ill, and he decided to move back to Caldmore to be closer to her; a decision which made us homeless. However, my uncle managed to persuade the landlord to allow us to move in with his mum at 29 Victor Street. The house was in a terrible condition because she was a very old lady and my mum cried for days because it was so awful. When the old lady passed away the landlord gave us the tenancy.

The house had three rooms upstairs and two downstairs rooms with a kitchen at the rear. The kitchen was very small but had to house an old brick boiler for washing, a Belfast sink and a gas cooker. The house was perfect

A meeting of the Caldmore Residents Action Group in the early 1970s.

for our needs, but it was just lacking those basic amenities. But I had a great feeling about living in Caldmore as I felt I belonged to everyone in the street as all the mums would look after each other's kids and I felt safe.

Dad was Bert Blower and a strong National Union of Railwaymen trade unionist. I remember he stopped me having the *Dandy* and *Beano* comics delivered because Thomson's who published them were non-union. I also remember at the end of the war fetching our first tin of fruit off rationing, a tin of pineapples, which us kids had been looking forward to but dad said 'you can't have these they are South African'. Both he and mum had strong principles.

One night in 1970 I got a knock on door and a bloke from the Labour Party was there. He said his name was Graham Rea and that he was standing for the Labour Party in Walsall South and he'd been let down by his agent. He said he had six weeks to go before the election and someone had told him that I might be able to help him to organise his campaign. I told him I wasn't a member of the Labour Party and he said he'd had my name given to him. So I asked my old man whether he thought I ought to do it and he said, 'yeah have a go at it'.

I found myself running a general election campaign with just six weeks to go. This brought me into the Labour Party where I met some very interesting people. At that time community action was becoming a big thing and Brian Powell who had lost a safe Labour seat was looking for an unwinnable seat like Caldmore to get his credibility back. Caldmore was at that time a safe Tory seat as the area was divided by a hill where on the one side were the poorer people who had given up the ballot box as a means of change whilst on the other was the 'landed gentry' of Highgate. And so it was always a safe Tory seat.

There was also a sociologist, a guy called Simon Major, who taught at the local technical college. He was writing a thesis on communities so his interest in seeing the people of Caldmore having a say in their future was important to him. Finally there was me, looking for an inside toilet and bathroom for my mum and dad. So in 1970 the three of us, each with our particular interest, decided to put out some leaflets inviting people to a public meeting to talk about the problem of housing in the Caldmore area.

Over a hundred people turned up to the meeting and we realised then just how deep the feelings were for change. At that meeting we formed the Caldmore Residents' Action Group and dad was elected as the first Chair and one of our neighbours was appointed Secretary and the group used our front room as its base.

The demolition of two Georgian houses in Doveridge Place in April 1974; thanks to the Express and Star. *Simon Major, of the Caldmore Residents Action Group, told a reporter that 'this is destroying vital units of accommodation. There was nothing structurally unsound with these two houses. They were not of great architectural or historical interest, but there was plenty of living accommodation there for four or five houses.'*

Through publicity we started to get a lot of local and national attention and people from Shelter in London came to see the work we were doing along with people from Cadbury Trust and the Gulbenkian Trust who gave us generous donations. With this money we were able to buy a small shop on Caldmore Green which we converted into an advice centre. However in order to receive these donations we needed to set up a new charity and so formed the Act Aid Trust.

I was still working at the power station, working shifts and so I had time off during the day to be involved at the advice centre. What we were doing would be the forerunner of the neighbourhood office concept. None of us were trained. All we were doing was articulating people's problems to the local authority or to whoever we needed to talk to. The advice centre became a neighbourhood meeting place and we picked up all kinds of problems that we never knew existed in our community. For example

Barrie's mum, Flo, on the right is with other women fundraising for the Action Group in the early 1970s.

women suffering violence, people with learning difficulties, people with mental health problems many of whom were getting no support.

In fact there was a whole range of social needs uncovered and we realised that we had got to do more than just offer advice. By 1972 the action group was very large, in fact it was the largest housing action group outside London. Every street in Caldmore had its own representative and they would collect sixpences off the people on Friday night in their respective streets so we could run off our news-sheet propaganda. The area was then divided into five different geographical areas each having their own committees and the chairpersons of these sat on the main Residents' Action Group Committee. These groups were right at the heart of the Caldmore community.

Through the national attention we were getting we were invited from time to time to talk about community action to various groups. On one occasion I went to speak at Warwick University and while I was there I met a guy called Alan Edgar who was running a housing association in Birmingham. I had never heard of these before but as he was talking I thought they would fit in perfectly with what we were trying to do in Caldmore.

After the meeting I invited him to see if Caldmore was a suitable area for us to set up a housing association. He came over and helped us to form a Board with local people which included the Principal of the West Midlands College who became our first Chair; local shopkeepers, residents and councillors. So by 1972 what we had in Caldmore was a political arm in Caldmore Residents' Action Group, a charitable arm in the Act Aid Trust managing the advice centre which was manned by volunteers and the provider in the housing association with the ability to provide new homes and improve the older stock. The advice centre became the headquarters of all three organisations and the three worked closely together.

Walsall Council recognised the benefit of such centres to the community so in the early 1980s they set up a local neighbourhood office network throughout the town. However because of the speed at which they had to set these offices up they were unable to identify local leaders from the communities and had to parachute in community and housing professionals. These had limited success as they were never able to connect with the local community in the same way.

Keeping People Together: Caldmore Housing Association

To get the housing association set up we needed some seed money so Simon Major and I went around the town to the various banks looking for support. The basic principle was that if you had a bank's support and that of the local authority, then you could attract loans and grants from the Government. However, it was at the time when banks were employing 'whizz kids' and the old-style bank managers were disappearing. Simon and I had a well-rehearsed patter to go in with but they just blanked us, asking where our collateral was and as we had none, they showed no interest in supporting us.

We didn't go to Barclays because they were still involved with apartheid in South Africa at the time but one night we decided to swallow our pride and make an appointment with them. We went to see this old guy at Barclays and gave him our patter – what it was all about, what we were trying to achieve, telling him his money was safe because it would be locked into property and so on. While we were talking, this guy never looked up once but sat there writing on his pad and even when we were leaving he never looked up. He said, 'I'll give you an answer tomorrow' which was at least better than the responses we had had before.

Next day we had this phone call – could we go down to see him. So we went down and he asked us what we needed. We stuttered £5000, which was a lot of money in those days and he said, 'right it'll be in a new account tomorrow, leave us your details'. Simon and I walked out stunned but we knew that we were on our way.

At our first AGM about eighteen months later this bank manager from Barclays came to the meeting. I told him that we had gone all round Walsall looking for bank support but nobody would give us any and asked him what did he see that they didn't? And he said, 'you only lend on two things – one is the idea sound and I thought your idea was, and secondly are these two people in front of me excited enough to make it work? I listened to you and thought yes these two guys will make it work.' He also told me he was due to retire shortly and could afford to take another risk so we obviously happened to be there at the right time.

At a meeting in the White Hart pub on Caldmore Green held in June 1972 the Caldmore Area Housing Association was officially formed from people who either lived in or had an interest in Caldmore. We bought our first two houses for refurbishment in Thorpe Road which cost £400 each. We then began to acquire properties around Caldmore and which still lacked basic amenities. The Council designated parts of Caldmore as General Improvement Areas and Housing Action Areas which started to bring more resources in.

If you have novices running around trying to do their best you can often rely on the professionals wanting to come and help and it was true in this case. We had bought our first 40 properties and were supposed to be

A festival scene in 1974; the Caldmore Housing Advice centre is to the left of the 'Baker's Arms' pub.

receiving Housing Association Grant but nothing arrived. The Department of the Environment sent a fellow over to find out how we were paying for these properties and he asked, 'have you claimed any grant?' We told him we were borrowing from Walsall MBC and wasn't aware that we hadn't claimed the grant.

The bloke was upset as he'd never heard of this before and we were breaking all the rules although we weren't doing it deliberately. He went back to the DoE and sent us some forms to claim what was then Revenue Deficit Grant and when this arrived it very nicely paid off all the loans on the properties we had acquired and improved up till then.

Our first new-build was a three-storey block of flats on the Birmingham Road on a nice piece of land sitting beside the canal and we decamped a large number of elderly people out of one of the streets in Caldmore where the houses were being demolished. This way they stayed together. We extended this idea when the Council were knocking properties down in other parts of Caldmore as we would try to move people together into new developments.

That's how the Action Group, the Advice Centre and the Housing Association were set up and the three people involved at the beginning were successful in achieving their own personal aims. Brian Powell won the Caldmore seat for Labour, Simon Major went off to be a producer with the BBC in London on the back of his thesis and, in 1976, mum and dad had their bathroom.

A Pioneer in Housing: Caldmore Housing

The Action Group declined by 1975/76 as many of the campaigns had been fought and it was hard to enthuse people to take up the fight on areas of activity that they couldn't directly identify with. The Advice Centre carried on in existence through to the early 1980s by which time Caldmore Housing had established itself as the focal point for the people in the area and took over their role. We still had tenants' groups and ensured that local people were still very much involved in our work.

As the Housing Association developed it very early on picked up on some of the problems that were coming though the Advice Centre. For example just before one Christmas a woman rang me from a phone box saying that her landlord had taken all the light bulbs out of the house she was in and they were in darkness. I went down to the house and this man, his wife and three children were in the attic room. When I opened the door the stench was awful. The room was lit by candles and the youngest child was in a cot with a net over it to stop the rats from jumping on her. I could not believe this. The landlord had taken out all of the light bulbs as a means of emptying the property to sell and these were his last remaining tenants.

I got onto BBC TV and Alan Towers, a news reporter, came over and he was great. He shot it all for TV and when it went out on the evening I got a call right away from the Chairman of the Walsall Housing Committee who asked if he could come and look at the property. It was a freezing cold night but we met – he and his wife were going out to some special occasion – he was dressed in black tie and she had a fur coat on. Nevertheless they went with me to the top of the stairs and once he had seen the conditions he said he would re-house them the next day. His wife also very generously gave them a ten bob note.

The following day he rang to say he had got a property in Bloxwich and could we move them there. We gathered together furniture from different sources and we moved the family in but kept going back as the couple also had learning difficulties and needed to have long-term support. A nice thing about this story is that I was walking through the town some years later and this girl came up to me and said, 'hello Barrie you don't remember me do you? Well I was only five', and she told me that she was one of the daughters who was in the attic room. She was now a sister in the hospital and the kids had all gone on to do well.

We had to recognise that some landlords in the area were treating their people very badly and we did a lot of work to expose them. We thought it might be problematical as a few of them were Indian landlords, mainly Sikhs but the local Sikhs in the community supported us and joined our campaign.

We also had the first women's refuge outside London where Erin Pizzey had formed the first in Chiswick in 1971. The local authority was providing no help for victims of domestic abuse; it remained hidden. However you do things out of necessity. I was in the Advice Centre one Friday night and a woman came knocking on the door with two kids and a carrier bag looking for help. She said her husband who was across the road had been hitting her and as he appeared rather drunk I fetched her in and locked the door.

I rang up the duty social services officer and said, 'I've got a lady here with two kids suffering violence – is there a safe home for her anywhere?' He said she did have somewhere to live and that they didn't have houses and it was obviously a housing problem, so speak to housing services. I rang up the duty housing officer who said they hadn't got any houses available and what's more it would be a social services problem where children are involved. So in the end I took her and the two kids late on Friday night down to our house to sleep in the front room.

On Saturday morning I rang up the Chairman of Social Services and explained the position of this family. He rang me back two hours later and said that they could go to The Shrubbery, which was a place for young girls having babies. He said they could stop there temporarily until it was sorted out. I went down there with this woman and her two kids but the lady who was in charge of The Shrubbery wasn't very happy to receive them but finally agreed.

After this argy bargy at about half past two in the afternoon I got a phone call from the mum crying saying, 'can you come down they're taking the kids off me'. When I got there this social worker was dragging the kids towards his car and when I intervened he threatened me with legal action. It would appear that he could legitimately take the kids into care for their protection and let the mother find somewhere for herself to live. This was apparently normal at that time – not just in Walsall but nationally.

So we lobbied the council for short-life properties that could be used as a refuge for victims of domestic violence. Our first schemes were some short-life properties in Caldmore and a large house on Mellish Road before moving to our present refuge on a permanent basis. It meant that we could keep the families together, get the kids into schools and then rehouse the families into somewhere safe.

As time went by we were able to meet a number of social needs for people who had either been ignored or neglected. The strength of the Caldmore community meant that newly-arriving immigrants from the Asian sub-continent and the Caribbean were able to be welcomed into the area. In some parts of the town there was an element of racial tension but not in Caldmore. Soon temples and mosques were springing up alongside existing churches to meet the religious needs.

We were aware of how important family life is for the Asian communities but due to the limitation on the size of many of the properties, large families were looking for a place of care for their elderly relatives. To meet this need we built Apna Ghar, a residential care scheme with a day centre attached and it continues to be in demand today.

We went on to work not only in Caldmore but also in other parts in and around Walsall town centre. We had to buy land wherever it was available but we tried to purchase this land within pram pushing distance of the office.

The whole thing about Caldmore Housing was that we were out of sync with the rest of the housing association movement at that time as they were still being run very much like local authority housing departments or private landlords. I remember giving a talk very early on at one of the National Housing Federation conferences and saying, 'the tenants own these properties as much as we do – they live there, pay their rent and look after them. Our job is just to manage and support them as they are not subordinate to us.' Many walked out of the meeting not wishing to listen to this line of thinking. It is satisfying now to see that tenants play a much greater role in the work of housing associations.

The opening of Apna Ghar in The Pleck in 1988. These were the first purpose-built dwellings for Asian elderly in the locality.

*HRH Diana, Princess of Wales, shaking hands with Caldmore Area Housing
Association chief executive Barrie Blower – and to his left is chairman Richard Newby.
The occasion was the opening of the Project for the Deaf in Lichfield Street in 1986.*

Caldmore at that time was a very self-contained area. It had its own
cinema, the old 'Forum', where our offices are now; five pubs; five churches;
and it was a thriving shopping area.

In the 1980s we were getting support from the local authority and the
government and were able therefore to develop new schemes to meet specific
needs. We built 120 single person units in Walsall town centre which were
officially opened by the Duke of Edinburgh and a deaf hostel which attracted a
visit from Princess Diana. We also developed a number of care schemes, many
of which started life in short-life properties before moving to permanent homes.

I became the Chief Executive of the association in 1972/73 and
remained in post for 30 years before retiring. It was hard work but I never
woke up any morning thinking I wasn't going to enjoy the day.

Creating Jobs: Caldmore Area Urban Support Enterprise

In 1980 large manufacturing companies, many of whom employed our
tenants, were closing down and the government set up the Manpower Services

Commission to offer short-term employment to people being displaced. One morning in 1980 an agent from the Manpower Services came to see us and asked if we could take some people on. He made it sound simple, saying, 'think of a scheme, set it up, create jobs and we'll support you financially'.

I devised a couple of schemes and we took on twenty people – adults who had recently been made redundant. That lasted for about six months before the chap came back and said, 'how would you like to do more of this?' I said yes and he then said, 'it's a bit difficult as I want you to find work for 500 adults and 120 kids – I've got to hit these targets and I've only got a couple of weeks to do it in'. So we agreed.

In order to get these schemes off the ground you had to get the local authority and respective trades unions' permission to ensure that none of these projects threatened permanent posts. I spent five days and nights writing up 22 different projects and within six weeks we had 500 adults working on a whole range of differing schemes such as Visiting the Elderly, an urban farm, a fun bus, talking news for the blind, laundry services, clearing public footpaths and so on. The men would work for six months, sometimes a year depending on what scheme they were on and then they had to go out and seek employment. It was satisfying to see that many who left the Visiting the Elderly scheme returned later on a voluntary basis to carry on with the people they were visiting.

Young people learning building skills on a Manpower Services Commission Scheme in 1982.

A spin-off for the men involved was that they were finding new interests and new talents they had never tested or tried before. In fact the murals that were painted by some of these men on the urban farm walls were really professional and these were men who had recently been pumping out nuts and bolts for GKN.

All was going well until the Housing Corporation, our regulator, reminded us that we were a housing provider and that we were operating contrary to our rules and acting ultra vires. They advised that we should set up a different company to carry out this work and we formed the Caldmore Area Urban Support Enterprise Ltd (Cause) of which I became Chief Executive to enable the two organisations to run in close harmony.

The Manpower Services Commission also supported us in providing 120 places for youths on what was then the Youth Training Scheme (YTS). The Council leased us a builder's yard where we provided training in motor mechanics, building, brick-laying, plastering, carpentry, painting and decorating. We had 125 youngsters all on one site and our ambition was to give them some good practical skills that they could take away with them. The Manpower Services Commission finished in the late 1980s but not before thousands of adults and young people had benefited from the Cause enterprises.

Ethos with Accord

Over the 40 years since Caldmore Housing started we had some influence on the housing association movement as we were able to demonstrate a different edge to its work by showing that it is the people who are the most important element in what we do. I was awarded the MBE in 1993 in recognition of our work and this was seen as an award for all the people involved in Caldmore Housing.

Caldmore Housing had been half of my working life and it allowed me to move into other circles. For example I always had an interest in health issues and I was made Chairman of the local hospital for three years. As a passionate football supporter, I was also thrilled to become involved with the Saddlers (Walsall FC) and even watched them reach the semi-finals of the then League Cup.

In 1986 plans were announced to move the club to Birmingham, a move to which I was strongly opposed and so I started a campaign to keep Walsall FC in Walsall. The campaign was successful and the Saddlers moved to a brand new ground in 1990, just down the road from Caldmore and still firmly part of the local community. I became Chairman of the club and am now very proud to be the life-long President, a part of the terrace and boardroom communities!

Today Caldmore Housing is run in a very similar way to my day with a Board and Chief Executive. The staff members are obviously more professional than when we first started but the culture and empathy within the organisation has never changed.

In our early times we built mainly in the Caldmore and town centre areas because when we were starting there were two other housing trusts operating from estate agents offices. One was working in the east of the Borough and the other in the west. Then in the early 1990s, Chris Handy joined Parklands Housing Association and within a couple of years this had merged with Walsall & District Housing Trust and Westland Housing Society to form the Accord Group.

Chris believed that in order to attract investment you needed to grow in size year on year. Our philosophy as a locally-based housing association providing for local needs limited our growth. Chris believed that you could stay local irrespective of how large you grew and of course this proved to be right. The culture of Accord is very much tenant-orientated and Chris is a

The signing ceremony at the Sister Dora Project in 1995 – a mixed tenure scheme of 98 units in partnership with Accord.

The 40th birthday celebration of Caldmore Area Housing Association in June this year. From the left Barrie Blower, Mike Hew Chief Executive Officer Caldmoreaccord, Bruce Gilbert, Chair of Caldmoreaccord, and former chair David Matthews.

great believer in social justice so when we were invited to join the Accord Group it was an easy decision for the Board to make. The Accord Group already had a number of associations attached to it; Ashram, bchs, Redditch Co-op Homes and it was the right time for Caldmore to join.

So we are now part of a bigger group doing a lot of new and exciting things both in the housing and community fields along with employment and health. Caldmore Housing can be proud of its history and I am sure its next 40 years as part of the Accord Group will be equally as productive.

Finally, on a personal note I must say that the history of Caldmore Housing could not have happened if it wasn't for a succession of excellent expert and knowledgeable boards led by effective chairs who helped to devise the strategies and then supported the executive in their execution. To them I owe a personal debt. Again, organisations which are people orientated need devoted caring staff who enjoy working in challenging situations and over the years we have been blessed with a plethora of these from which our tenants have been the beneficiaries.

Finally, the residents of Caldmore and the tenants of Caldmore Housing Association have also played a major role in the work we have done and long may that be the case – that community has been at the heart of my own life for so long and vital to Caldmore for the future.

Chapter 10

MAKING A REAL DIFFERENCE: DIRECT HEALTH

Jonathan Vellacott, Chief Executive Direct Health

Direct Health is one of the UK's leading providers of care to people in their own homes and it is a business which has enjoyed solid and organic growth. It has an excellent reputation both for the quality of its care and for its strength as a business, and it is fully-integrated into the communities in which it operates.

Currently, Direct Health has eighteen branches across the Midlands, North East and North West regions from its head office in Nottingham. It delivers a broad range of services which are provided to older people, young adults, children and families. These services cover both social and personal care and increasingly more specialist healthcare services. In fact Direct Health provides approximately 50,000 hours of care a week to a core base of around 6,000 customers.

Starting in Derbyshire, the company has provided care to people in their own homes since 1995. Having gained a good reputation, the company expanded into Nottinghamshire, Leicestershire and across South Yorkshire. Direct Health continued to expand under the ownership of a Chesterfield born and bred entrepreneur who also founded Auto Windscreens in the 1960s.

It was in 2003 that I took over the running of the company. At that time Direct Health employed 250 staff, had a turnover of £4 million and was providing domiciliary care to approximately 600 people. I realised that Direct Health had the opportunity to make a positive difference to people's lives and their ability to live independently.

Chris Handy OBE, Chief Executive of Accord Group, shaking hands with Jonathan Vellacott, Chief Executive of Direct Health.

Since then Direct Health has grown significantly. It currently employs 2,500 staff, has a turnover of £32 million and provides services to more than 6,500 people. In 2005, Direct Health acquired At Your Service, the largest provider of domiciliary care in Nottinghamshire, and a year later we acquired Verna Community Care, which had several branches across the Midlands and the North.

Alongside these acquisitions Direct Health has also grown organically, providing services to more people in the communities we have traditionally served whilst also expanding into neighbouring communities and regions. This growth has resulted from strong staff training, robust recruitment and clear and concise management processes.

Making sure that we provide care and support services of the highest quality, individually planned, will enable Direct Health to be a preferred provider for the people in the communities that we serve. In order to achieve this, we have to look after our staff and be an employer of choice.

We ensure that our staff are competent in the roles that they perform and celebrate their outstanding achievements. Many staff in different roles have not only been nominated for the Great British Care Awards at a regional level but have gone on to win regional and national awards.

I believe that the future of Direct Health will be one of continued organic growth, especially as the demand for domiciliary care grows. This will be achieved by delivering care in Direct Health's existing communities and expanding into neighbouring areas. We are also keen to broaden the range of care services offered by expanding into more specialist services such as end-of-life services and care to those with spinal or brain injuries.

More and more people are living longer and requiring care in their homes to remain independent. The current system relies on a high level of state provision but as local government resources will continue to be under pressure, we need to look for communities to be more self-sustainable in providing for their needs. Through joining the Accord Group in the summer of 2012, Direct Heath will be able to offer communities across the Midlands and the North increased access to a broader range of care and support services in the comfort of their own homes.

There is a synergy between Direct Health and the Accord Group's services because both are tailored to the needs of the individual and have emphasised independence, choice, respect, dignity and fulfilment for residents. Although the Group has been able to offer residential schemes, it also recognises the importance of 'floating' support, so that people can receive the care they need in the comfort and privacy of their own homes.

Direct Health will extend the Accord Group's scope and geographical reach in this side of the business, and it will enable the Group to broaden its provision of higher acuity care. In fact we expect that the Group will approximately double its health and social care turnover. It will also increase the reach of its care services by allowing it to provide around 3.5 million hours of home-based and residential care each year. Above all the aim is to enable people to lead independent lives.

Direct Health will continue to operate as an independent company with all the benefits of being part of the larger Accord Group. Direct Health is a solid and well regarded operator within the domiciliary care sector. I believe that becoming part of the Accord Group will enable us to provide a broader range of services into the communities that we serve. We believe that this solid base will allow us, with Accord's support, to accelerate Direct Health's growth; focusing specifically on geographical expansion, a broadening of the care offering into higher acuity services and acquisition of further complex care capability.

ENDWORD

Dr Chris Handy OBE

Although Accord has a history and contribution to society it can be proud of, we cannot rest there. There is still so much to do. We are a family of organisations, each one having made real positive differences to the life chances of the people we've helped and supported over our collective histories. In all we have existed for well over 200 years. Our oldest group member is Fry Housing Trust which was formed in 1959 in memory of the terrific work of Margery Fry the penal reformer. As part of this work I looked back on her contribution. She was a polyglot, pioneering so many things, the reform of prisons and the treatment of prisoners just one of her interests.

In a sense, though, we go back much further than the 1950s! We support a number of almshouse charities all but one of which was formed during the Victorian period to provide housing as a means of "alms" to the poor. One of these almshouse charities, Harpers in Walsall, was formed as far back as the twelfth century. Our links to important work in housing people in need can be tracked back to medieval times.

This is all quite a legacy but not enough when there are growing needs in society. We have to accelerate our work over the coming years. I believe we have always been a force for good, making a positive difference and we must enlarge that work in the future. Yes providing housing, health and social care. But also helping people find work, helping to spark special movements in the communities we serve, helping people to start their own enterprises, helping to create social capital and tackling social injustice.

In some ways the people who work in Accord, managing and leading it, and our Board members who do the vital work of overseeing the entire work of the Group, are custodians of the Group's work. We're passing through, but the work goes on uninterrupted. As we've been writing the history it's made me think of those people who've made a really big contribution over the years and who are no longer involved. Dr John Griffith, Maurice Wolverson, Betty Deakin and Phil Wood all big contributors, each of them chairing the Boards of Management of the Group and its member organisations. There have been others too. I recall Connie Dutton one of our tenants who was involved in the work of one of the associations for over twenty years in different ways.

This is important, our work can never stop. New people have taken on the role and we've got some terrific people now heading up our Boards. We've had a succession of brilliant chairmen who have given their time and commitment to the work we do, steered and challenged and made the work accountable. Tony Green, Derek Leyland, Barry Picken and our present Chair, Akshay Parikh, have all given so much and taken the Group to new heights. All of them have been ambitious for the Group and been completely dedicated to our mission of meeting housing, health and support needs.

We have great staff working here who help to deliver services on the ground. Their jobs going forward are changing. We're expecting a new approach in the coming months and years helping our customers into work, improving their financial positions where we can, helping people form their own enterprises and making a real contribution to local communities through such initiatives as AddVentures and Locality for Real. Obviously I must thank them for all the dedicated and skilled work they do.

Staff come and go too of course and some who have left need a mention; Gerry Cornell who led Westland Homes and was so dedicated and hard-working; Dave Cusack and Tracey Rowe for all of their important work with Moseley and District; Jon Stevens, Ursula Barrington and Ruth Miller for leading bchs and their dedication to mutual housing; Clive Childs for his work with Walsall and District and Frank Bailey for his leadership of Fry Housing Trust to name but a few. But you have to admire those who have stuck things out and continued to play an important role. Wendy Powell, Sally McCready and Jane Irwin have all worked for us, for an extraordinary 30 years.

But most importantly, I can never thank our tenants enough. Those who get involved in what we do, challenging us and helping us make our services meaningful and of the highest quality, all have helped us make this Group what it is. Many thanks to Kath Hodson for all of her work. And also Adam Jenkins, Barbara Timmins, Janet Payne, Peter Tonks, Anne Harborne, Joy Kirby-Tibbetts again to name but a few. All of the tenant board members on bchs and RCH, they show us outstanding leadership. All of the tenant groups and co-ops who stand behind them and run their own communities, making their own decisions and constantly showing housing professionals how to do the job better.

Some of the partnerships we've formed with tenants and community groups have been very strong too. Bob Bone and Kerry Lee of Bushbury Triangle have been a formidable partnership, a great team who have worked wonders for their community. And I have to mention the great Terry Edis who chaired bchs for many years and who sadly passed way in 2011 and who was Chair of WATMOS a key partner of ours. Terry was the epitome of the tenant movement in this country … a very sad loss to all who knew him.

And now is the time to pick up the pace, do more than we have done before. Despite the 'Cathy Come Home' origins of some of our Group members, homelessness still exists. It has changed its face and its nature but this problem continues. Who would think that in an advanced civilised society, a twenty-first century Britain that the fundamental need of a person to have their own home would continue to go unmet. A home ought to be a fundamental human right and yet people become and remain homeless, street homelessness grows and along with it, that other scourge of modern society (and a disgrace for us all), child poverty, is increasing yet again. And for our family, the Accord family, which was born in part to tackle the breakdown of families, tackling these issues is a core propelling emotion.

So we must build more! We can never build enough housing for people. We must do more! Our waiting lists and those of our partners, local authorities, are growing due to the shortage of housing and the inability of the housing sector to meet new demands generated by significant demographic change.

We are well prepared. In our own right we are a significant housing provider with more than 11,000 properties providing services to over 50,000 customers. We are financially strong with a turnover in excess of £100m a year, assets at open market value of over £1bn, a development programme of over £30m a year building more homes, employing close on 4,500 people and delivering over 3.5m hours of home care to people so they can live independently in their own homes.

This last aspect of our work has been helped by Direct Health, a private sector care company in the Group, which specialises in domiciliary care working in the Midlands and North. We have our own factory, LoCaL Homes, building high quality low carbon timber homes. It manufactures one home per day and we have the capacity to increase this to three homes per day. The homes are incredibly warm and cost very little to heat, even in the coldest of winter months, reducing energy bills at a time when these have continued to rise and rise.

Equally, we have been innovative in raising funding to build new homes. We're looking at new and exciting ways to continue to do this to maximise our impact, addressing housing need and homelessness. Working with other Matrix Partners – a wider partnership of housing associations working in the Midlands and South West – we are building over 2,000 homes over the next few years with more to come.

We have a strong offer in the provision of health and social care through Accord itself and Direct Health. The needs of an ageing population will rise over the coming years. We are well placed to provide an outstanding range of services to people so they can live independently. And there's a link here to employment for our tenants and members of their families. We are such a big employer with a solid future that we can provide a number of career pathways, care and support is just one of these many opportunities. In health and social care alone we employ over 3,500 people.

And our mixed economy approach – a mixture of traditional housing association along with private sector profit making activities – enables us to make money and plough this back into our core purpose of meeting housing, health and social care needs.

The challenge lies ahead and we are confident of meeting that. With our Boards, our staff, our partners and customers we are able to make a formidable contribution.

Chris Handy